Labour Law in China

Labour Law in China

Second Edition

Chen, Ke

This book was originally published as a monograph in the International Encyclopaedia of Laws/Labour Law and Industrial Relations.

Founding Editor: Roger Blanpain
General Editor: Frank Hendrickx
Volume Editor: Frank Hendrickx

Wolters Kluwer

Published by:
Kluwer Law International B.V.
PO Box 316
2400 AH Alphen aan den Rijn
The Netherlands
E-mail: international-sales@wolterskluwer.com
Website: lrus.wolterskluwer.com

Sold and distributed in North, Central and South America by:
Wolters Kluwer Legal & Regulatory U.S.
7201 McKinney Circle
Frederick, MD 21704
United States of America
Email: customer.service@wolterskluwer.com

Sold and distributed in all other countries by:
Air Business Subscriptions
Rockwood House
Haywards Heath
West Sussex
RH16 3DH
United Kingdom
Email: international-customerservice@wolterskluwer.com

Printed on acid-free paper

ISBN 978-94-035-0305-9

e-Book: ISBN 978-94-035-0185-7
web-PDF: ISBN 978-94-035-0270-0

Printed in the United Kingdom.

The Author

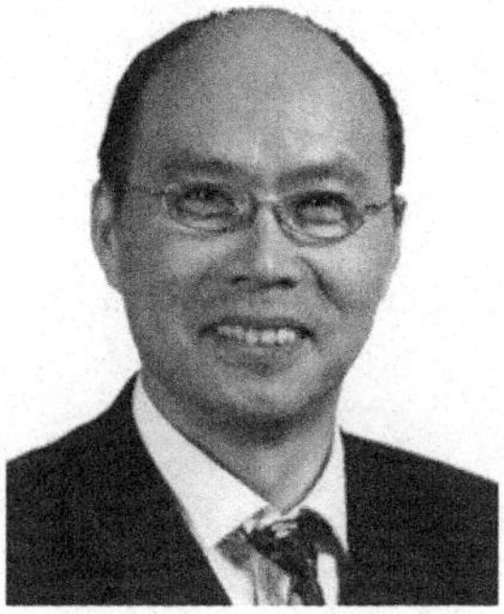

Chen, Ke received his LLB, and LLM degrees in Shanghai (1979–1986) and his PhD degree in law in Beijing (1987–1992). He was a Visiting Research Fellow at the University of Melbourne, Australia (1989–1990), at the Max Planck Institute for Foreign and International Social Law, Germany (1993–1994). He was a visiting professor at the Catholic University of Leuven, Belgium (autumn 1995). In the summer of 1994, he worked for the International Labour Organization in Geneva. He has practised Chinese commercial law in European law firms for many years. Currently, he is a senior partner of AllBright Law Offices, Shanghai, China. His mail address is chenke@allbrightlaw.com.

The author thanks Ms Dawen Gu for her assistance in research and comments on the current updated version of the monograph.

The Author

Table of Contents

List of Abbreviations

PRC	People's Republic of China
NPC	National People's Congress
CPC	Communist Party of China
ACFTU	All-China Federation of Trade Unions
CEDA	China Enterprise Directors' Association
CEA	China Enterprises Association

Introduction

Chapter 1. General Background

§1. Geography and Population

1. The People's Republic of China is situated in the eastern part of Asia, on the west coast of the Pacific Ocean. It has a territory of 9.6 million square kilometres. To the east, China borders Korea; to the north Mongolia; to the north-east Russia; to the north-west Kazakhstan, Kirghizia and Tadzhikistan, to the west and south-west Afghanistan, Pakistan, India and Nepal, Sikkim and Buhtan, to the south Myanmar, Laos and Vietnam.

2. According to the latest statistics of the Sixth National Population Census in 2010, including the population of Hong Kong, Macao and Taiwan, China has a total population of 1,370,536,875. The population in the mainland in 31 provinces, autonomous regions, municipalities directly under the central government and active servicemen is 1,339,724,852.[1] Compared with the statistics of the fifth National Population Census in 2000, the population has increased by 5.84 per cent in ten years, at an annual average of 0.57 per cent. China has maintained a low fertility rate in the past decade.

Of the population of 31 provinces, autonomous regions, municipalities directly under the central government and active servicemen, the Han population is 1,225,932,641, accounting for 91.51 per cent; the minority population is 113,792,211 people, accounting for 8.49 per cent. Compared with the fifth National Census in 2000, the Han population increased by 5.74 per cent, and the population of ethnic minorities increased by 6.92 per cent. Compared with the fifth National Census in 2000, the urban population increased by 13.46 per cent, up to 49.68 per cent; the population over 60 years of age increased by 2.93 per cent, up to 13.26 per cent.

1. See Bulletin of the Main Data of the Sixth National Population Census in 2010 (No. 1), by the National Bureau of Statistics of PR China, 28 April 2011

§2. HISTORY

3. The establishment of the Qin Dynasty in 221 BC ended the rivalry among the independent principalities in the warring state period and established the first centralized, unified, unitary state in Chinese history. Subsequently, the empire power was replaced by one dynasty after another. They included the Han Dynasty (206 BC–AD 220), Wei (220–265) and Jin (265–420), Southern and Northern Dynasties (420–589), Sui Dynasty (581–618), Tang Dynasty (618–907), Five Dynasty (907–960), Song Dynasty (960–1279), Ynan Dynasty (1271–1368), Ming Dynasty (1368–1644) and Qing Dynasty (1644–1911).

4. After the Qing government had lost the Opium War of 1840 against Britain and subsequent to the signing of the Nanking Treaty with Britain in 1842, Chinese national sovereignty was bartered away. This marked the reduction of China to a so-called 'semi-colonial and semi-feudal' country. The republican revolution of 1911 ended the rule of the Qing Dynasty and thus two thousand years of despotic bureaucracy in China.

5. However, war and revolution have never ended since the provisional government of the Republic of China in Peking was founded in 1911. From 1911 to 1927, China was torn by civil war between the 'warlords' supported by foreign powers. In 1916 Canton's revolutionary government, led by Dr Sun Yan-Sen, founder of the Republic, was set up in the south of China.

6. In 1919 the 4 May movement against imperialism and the Peking government took place. In this movement, the Chinese working class appeared for the first time on the political scene and showed its great strength and its potential role in the contemporary history of China. In 1921 the Chinese Communist Party was founded and allied itself in 1924 with Dr Sun Yan-Sen's Nationalist Party to take part in an expedition northward against the warlords (1924–1927). Chiang Kai-Shek succeeded after Dr Sun Yan-Sen's death in 1925 and started a war against the Communist Party in 1927 until 1937 when both parties and their armed forces reunited in order to resist the Japanese invasion during World War II (1939–1945). Civil war (1945– 1949) broke out between Nationalist Party and Communist Party armed forces after the Japanese surrender. The Communist Party's armed forces won the war and the Nationalists retreated to Taiwan. On 1 October 1949, Mao Tse-Tung, Chairman of the Communist Party, proclaimed the founding of the People's Republic of China.

7. Massive political campaigns and economic construction had been the main themes since the 1950s. The failure of the Great Leap Forward towards the establishment of an ideal communist society at the end of the 1950s was followed a few years later by the Great Cultural Revolution which lasted for ten years (1966–1976). It was not until Mao's death in 1976 and the subsequent prosecution of his wife and three other members of the so-called Gang of Four that the man-made 'massive class struggle' ended and dramatic ideological and social change took place. Since the end of 1978 China had been determined to rebuild its socialist legal order as well as to modernize its economy by adopting the policy of opening up to the outside world. After decades of economic and limited political reform, the so-called 'socialist market economy' was endorsed by a constitutional amendment in 1993.[2]

§3. The Political System

8. The practice of market-oriented, decentralized economic reform, adopted at the Third Plenary Session of the 11th Central Committee of the Communist Party of China (CPC) in December 1978, called for a democratic, institutionalized, political and social system to be regulated by a sound and stable legal system. The 1982 Constitution[3] provided a constitutional basis for the establishment of a political system which intended to tackle the problems such as the weakness of the people's representative system, excessive concentration of power in the Communist Party of China, patriarchies, lifelong tenure in official posts and abuse of privilege, etc. The existing Constitution with its 1988, 1993, 1999, 2004 and 2018 amendments also placed emphasis on the protection of individual rights and the promotion of effective citizen participation in state management and economic activities. The Constitution has become the flag for performance of duties and responsibilities by the state organizations, public institutions and civil servants.

9. China is a multinational, unitary state with 23 provinces (including Taiwan), 5 autonomous regions, 4 municipalities directly under the central government and Hong Kong and Macao, which are special administrative regions, which have capitalist systems and practise the policy of 'one country two systems'. The nature of the state is stipulated in Article 1 of the Constitution as a socialist state under the 'People's Democratic Dictatorship' led by the working class and based on the alliance of workers and peasants. The legitimate political philosophy, explicitly stipulated in the preamble to the Constitution, is the 'Four Cardinal Principles' namely, adherence to the socialist road, to the People's Democratic Dictatorship, to leadership of the Communist Party of China, and to Marxism, Leninism, and Mao Tse-Tung's thought. The 1989 student-led protests provoked a political crisis which made authorities view political reform as a long-term strategy rather than an overnight revolution. The collapse of the East European socialist regimes followed in 1991 by the dissolution of the Soviet Union further convinced China of the need to move towards a less politically authoritarian system and a more socially and economically pluralist system.

10. The form of the political system in accordance with Article 2 of the Constitution is the system of people's congress. Article 2 says all power in the People's

2. See *Zhonghua Renmin Gongheguo Guowuyuan Gongbao* (Gazette of the State Council of the PRC), 8 July 1993, No. 10 at p. 416.
3. See Constitution of the PRC in *The Laws of the People's Republic of China* (1979–1982), Foreign Languages Press, Beijing, 1987 at p. 3. The latest English version of the Constitution of PRC can be found on the website Pkulaw.com.

Republic of China belongs to the people. The organs through which the people exercise state power are the National People's Congress and the local people's congresses at various levels. The establishment and the operation of the political system follow the constitutional principles of the people's congress system and democratic centralism. They are indicated by the following three aspects.

11. First, the National People's Congress and the local people's congresses at town, county and provincial levels are created by democratic election and are responsible to the people and subject to their supervision. The constituencies and the electoral units have the power to recall the representatives elected by them. Members of people's congresses at the county level and below are directly elected on the basis of universal suffrage. Members of people's congresses above the county level are indirectly elected, as they are elected by the people's congresses at the next lower level (Art. 97 of the Constitution). Citizens who have reached the age of 18 have the right to vote and stand for election, except those who have been deprived of their political rights (Art. 34 of the Constitution). The National People's Congress is the highest organ of state power, composed of the representatives elected in proportion to their population by the provinces, autonomous regions and municipalities directly under the central government and by the armed forces.

12. Secondly, the people's congresses can and should exercise state power in a unified way. The people's congresses presumably represent the will and interest of the people to formulate the laws and policies through democratic procedures. All the other state organs are established, and their powers are authorized, by the people's congress. The state administrative organs (the State Council at the national level and people's governments at local levels), the adjudicative organs (the Supreme People's Court, the Local People's Courts and Special Courts) and the prosecutorial organs or organs for legal supervision (the Supreme People's Procuratorates, the Local People's Procuratorates and Special Procuratorates) are created by the people's congresses, and are responsible to them and subject to their supervision at the corresponding level. Furthermore, at national level, the President of the state and the Chairman of the Central Military Commission are elected by the National People's Congress and are responsible to it and subject to its supervision.

13. Thirdly, the division of functions and powers between central and local authorities follows the principle of giving full play to the initiative and enthusiasm of local authorities under the unified leadership of the central authorities. The Constitution establishes that, under national law, the people's congresses and their standing committees in the provinces, autonomous regions and municipalities directly under the central government have the power to enact and promulgate local laws according to their specific condition.

14. The existing Constitution with its 1988, 1993, 1999, 2004 and 2018 amendments highlights not only the importance of improvement and strengthening of the people's congress system, but also the necessity of separating the state and the political parties. The activities of all political parties, including the Communist

Party, are duty bound to uphold the dignity of the Constitution and ensure its implementation, as the preamble to the Constitution calls for all political parties and other organizations to take the Constitution as the basic standard of conduct. No party and organization should equate itself with the state and act outside the Constitution (Art. 5 of the Constitution).

15. The political party system is expressed as a 'multiparty cooperation and political consultation system under the leadership of the Communist Party of China', words which were added to the preamble to the Constitution in the 1993 constitutional amendment. The Chinese People's Political Consultative Conference is the institution through which the Communist Party holds consultations with the eight officially recognized democratic political parties and other patriotic personages. The eight democratic political parties are the China Revolutionary Committee of the Nationalist Party, the China Democratic League, the China Democratic National Construction Association, the China Association for Promoting Democracy, the Chinese Peasants' and Workers' Democratic Party, the China Zhi Gong Dang, the Jiu San Society and the Taiwan Democratic Self-Government League.

As prescribed by the Constitution of the Chinese People's Political Consultative Conference, this is a system for carrying out political democracy in line with the policy of 'long-term coexistence and mutual supervision between the Communist Party and democratic parties' and other patriotic personages without party affiliation. The Chinese People's Political Consultative Conference establishes a national committee and local committee. The National Committee of the Chinese People's Political Consultative Conference holds a plenary session once every year to consult on major state policies and other issues concerning important aspects of people's lives, to provide suggestions and criticism.

16. The President of the People's Republic of China represents the state in its domestic and international affairs. The President and Vice-president are elected by the National People's Congress. Citizens of the People's Republic of China who have the right to vote and to stand for election and who have reached the age of 45 are eligible for election as President or Vice-president of the People's Republic of China. The term of office of the President and Vice-president is the same as that of the National People's Congress according to the 2018 amendments to the Constitution. In pursuance of the decisions of the National People's Congress and its Standing Committee, the President promulgates laws, appoints and removes most members of the State Council, confirms state medals and titles of honour, issues orders of special pardons, proclaims martial law, proclaims a state of war and issues mobilization orders. The President receives foreign diplomatic representatives on behalf of the state and, in pursuance of decisions of the Standing Committee of the National People's Congress, appoints and recalls plenipotentiary representatives abroad, and ratifies and abrogates treaties and important agreements concluded with foreign states. The Vice-president assists in the work of the President and may exercise such part of the functions and powers of the President as may be entrusted to him by the President.

17. The State Council is responsible for the enforcement of the laws and the decisions adopted by the National People's Congress and its Standing Committee. The State Council applies the system of decision by the Premier and the ministries and the commissions apply the system of decision by their respective Ministers. The Premier has overall responsibility for the State Council, and the Vice-premiers and the State Councillors assist in the work of the Premier. The State Council is also composed of the Ministers in charge of the ministries or commissions, the Auditor-General and the Secretary-General. The Premier convenes and chairs the executive meetings and plenary meetings of the State Council. The term of office of the State Council is the same as that of the National People's Congress. The functions and powers of the State Council, among others, are to formulate administrative regulations, to direct all administrative work of national character, including drawing up and implementing the national economic and social plan and the state budget, to exercise unified leadership over the work of the Ministers and commissions as well as that of local administration, and to exercise such other functions and powers as may be authorized by the National People's Congress and its Standing Committee.

18. The Central Military Commission is established by the Constitution to lead the armed forces of the country; thus the status of the armed forces in the state structure is defined. Building the armed forces is still the responsibility of the State Council. The Central Military Commission applies the system of decision by its Chairman. The Chairman of the Central Military Commission is elected and recalled by the National People's Congress. The term of the office of the Central Military Commission is the same as that of the National People's Congress. However, no limitation on the number of consecutive terms the Chairman may serve is stipulated in the Constitution. The latest amendments to the Constitution in 2018 also set no limitation on the number of consecutive terms of office of the President and Vice-president.

19. The judicial organs include the people's courts, the people's prosecutor and the public security organs. These three organs are required to divide functions but coordinate their work and check with each other to ensure correct and effective enforcement of the law (Art. 135 of the Constitution).

The court system consists of the Supreme People's Court, higher courts at provincial level, intermediate people's court in cities and prefectures within provinces and basic-level people's courts at county level. The system of two levels of review, with the second level as the final level, is practised, so the structure of people's courts as a whole comprises a system of two instances of review at four levels. In addition, there are also special courts such as military courts, railway transport courts and the maritime courts. The Supreme People's Court is the highest adjudicative organ which exercises appellate jurisdiction as well as original jurisdiction in important cases at national level. It has a supervisory function over the lower courts and has power to approve the death penalty. Its judicial interpretation provides general rules for courts to follow in adjudicating specific cases.

The operation of the court in its judicial work is fully reflected by the principle of collective leadership rather than the independence of an individual judge. A court is considered as a collective entity enjoying an independence and freedom from interference by the other state organs. People's courts set up adjudicative committees at all levels which are comprised of the President, Vice-president, chief judges and other judges of the court. The major functions of the adjudicative committee are to sum up judicial experience and to discuss major or difficult cases as well as other issues regarding judicial work. The people's assessors are invited or elected to join a collegiate bench for a trial at first instance. The members of a collegiate bench enjoy equal rights. For appeal cases, the collegiate bench does not include assessors as members. In trials of important and difficult cases heard by a collegiate bench, it is first required that the case be discussed by the adjudicative committee; the decision of the committee shall be implemented in granting the judgment by the collegiate bench (Art. 11 of the Organic Law of the People's Court, Art. 107 of Criminal Procedure Law of the People's Republic of China).

The structure of the people's prosecutorial office basically corresponds to that of the people's courts. But a prosecutor is not only subject to supervision of the people's congress at the same level, but also subject to vertical leadership of the prosecutor at the next highest level. As the legal supervisory organs of the state, the people's prosecutors are responsible for approving arrests made by public security organs, initiating public prosecutions, investigating crimes committed by officials, supervising court work by way of protesting against first instance decisions and supervising the activities of the public security organs and prisons (Art. 5 of the Organic Law of the People's Prosecutors).

The public security organs at various levels organized under the Ministry of Public Security are responsible for investigation, detention and preliminary examination in criminal cases. They also have the function of maintaining public order. It is worth noticing that the National Supervisory Commission as a special agency is set up under the 2018 amendments to the Constitution consolidating forces to combat the systematic corruption found in the party-state machinery.

20. The presidents of various courts at various levels are elected by people's congresses at the corresponding levels. Vice-presidents, chief judges of divisions, associate chief judges of divisions and judges are appointed and removed by the standing committee of the people's congresses at the corresponding levels. Members of the adjudicative committee of people's courts at various levels are nominated by the presidents of the courts to the standing committees of the corresponding people's congresses for appointment or removal. Generally, the chief prosecutors of the people's prosecutorial office at various levels are elected and removed by people's congresses at the corresponding levels. Deputy chief prosecutors, prosecutors and members of the prosecutorial committee of the people's prosecutorial office at various levels are nominated by the chief prosecutors to the standing committees of the corresponding people's congresses for appointment or removal.

21. All state organs are organized in a hierarchical structure. At the apex is the national or central level, and then the local level which includes provinces, prefectures or cities of prefectural rank, counties or cities of county rank and townships and the town level. Regional autonomy, consisting of autonomous regions, autonomous prefectures and autonomous counties, is practised in areas where minorities live in compact communities, where self-government is exercised pursuant to the Law of the People's Republic of China on Regional National Autonomy of 1984. The Hong Kong and Macao Special Administrative Regions, established under two decisions of the National People's Congress made in 1990 and 1993 respectively, are governed by the Basic Law of the Hong Kong Special Administrative Region and the Basic Law of the Macao Special Administrative Region.

§4. Economy

22. The 1993 constitutional amendments declared that China practises a socialist market economy. The 1999 constitutional amendments further declared that China would develop its socialist market economy and maintain various economic ownership systems. Under the existing Constitution, a legal framework for economic activities has been established and developed. State macro regulation and controls are emphasized, rather than administrative directives, as used to be in the old Soviet-style planned economies. The 1993 amendment also changed the wording 'state economy' to 'state-owned economy'. This change aims to accelerate the separation of ownership and management in state-owned enterprises. Ownership by the whole people and collective ownership by the working people are considered as the basis of the socialist economic system in China. According to Article 7 of the Constitution, the state-owned economy, i.e. the socialist economy with ownership by people as a whole, is the leading force in the national economy. The rural contracted responsibility system based mainly on the household linking remuneration to output and cooperative economic forms – producers' supply and marketing, credit and the consumers' cooperatives – are part of the socialist economy, collectively owned by the working people (Art. 8 of the Constitution). In addition, the 'individual economy' is regarded as a supplement to the socialist public economy. The private economy is constitutionally recognized. The existing Constitution recognizes and protects the legitimate rights of private property (Art. 13 of the Constitution) and permits the transfer of the land use right according to law by virtue of the 1988 constitutional amendment (Art. 10 of the Constitution). The sector of the economy with foreign participation in various forms is also constitutionally protected.

23. Towards the end of the 1970s, China's economic reform began with the dissolution of the commune system in the countryside and the adopting of the household responsibility system to revitalize peasants' initiatives on their own family contracted land. In the last four decades, Chinese peasants have been able to feed themselves with the harvest generated from their long-term contracted collectively owned land. Reform in the city was followed by the establishment of special economic zones along the coastal areas to test the liberal open-door policy, and promote experiences gained nationwide. In industry, the state-owned enterprises have been gradually granted decision-making power with regard to operations within the limits prescribed by the law and regulations. Since the beginning of the 1990s state-owned enterprises have gone through restructuring, forming companies limited by liability or companies limited by shares according to state regulations and company law, while others have gone into bankruptcy in accordance with the Bankruptcy Law. A contract system extracted from experiences in rural reform has been introduced into all fields of economic activity, including employment relationships. The economic reforms were further carried out in state-owned enterprises, finance, investment, fiscal policy and trade during the 1990s along with the establishment of rule by law at national, provincial and local level. The Chinese Communist Party had expected that China's modernization drive would be a great success, with its strategy anticipating that a 'socialist market economy' structure would be in place by the year 2000.[4] China has been creative in merging big and even contradictory concepts under one socialism theme. It has proved that the overwhelming forces generated by the market mechanism and contracting practice are effectively facilitating China's modernization.

Since China joined the World Trade Organization in 2001, Chinese economic reform had been put on an international footing. For the purpose of further driving economic growth, the 16th National Congress of the CPC, held in November 2002, called for building up a so-called 'well-off society', a term popular among Chinese farmers and peasants or mass society. This new domestic political theme is the reason for continuous effort to seek fortune and prosperity in the 21st century.[5]

The 19th CPC National Congress held in October 2017 declared that socialism with Chinese characteristics has entered a new era. It has drawn up a two-stage development plan for the period from 2020 to the middle of the 21st century to turn China into a great modern socialist country which will be prosperous, democratic, culturally advanced, harmonious and beautiful. It appears that China is also inclined to play its active role in reshaping universal values for the international community. The 2018 amendments to the Constitution mirrored all the key programmes proclaimed in the 19th CPC National Congress.

24. From 1979 to 1993 China's GNP has been growing at an annual average rate of about 14 per cent.[6] China has turned out to be one of the fastest growing nations in the Asia-Pacific region. According to the *World Bank Atlas 1995*, China's GNP in 1993 accounted for US$581.1 billion. However, China's per capita GNP in 1993 was only at US$490.[7] According to the data from the World Bank official website, China's GDP in 2006 accounted for US$2,668.1 billion. In 2016, Chinese GNI reached US$11,393.5 billion according to Word Bank data 2017. Meanwhile, the Chinese government has found it increasingly difficult to deal with the inflationary pressure caused by the overheated growth of the economy on the one h,.and and the growing social gap and hence social unrest as the side effect of development on the other hand.

---

4. CPC Central Committee Proposal for Economic Development, in *Beijing Review*, 13–19 November 1995.
5. Jian Defines Theme of CPC Congress, in *China Daily*, 9 November 2002.
6. See *Statistical Yearbook of Public Finance of China 1994*, at p. 443.
7. The *World Bank Atlas 1995*, at p. 18.

§5. EMPLOYMENT

25. The *1993 Statistical Yearbook* of China indicates that employment in the sector of state-owned enterprises and organization industry was 108.9 million persons and in the municipal collective sector was 36.2 million persons at the end of 1992. Due to economic restructuring, China's private economy is growing. According to Reuters, China boasted 654,000 private firms at the end of 1995, employing 8.22 million people.[8] The urban unemployment rate is officially reported as 2.9 per cent with 4.8 million people unemployed at the end of 1994,[9] and the character of unemployment in the cities normally takes a disguised form. In the rural areas, it mostly takes the form of underemployment. China, like other developing countries, gathers no unemployment statistics for rural areas.

The National Statistics Bureau of China indicates that employment in the sector of state-owned enterprises and organization industry dropped from 81.02 million persons by 2000 to 62.08 million by 2015; from 14.99 million to 4.81 million in the municipal collective sector respectively. On the other hand, employment of foreign investment companies increased significantly from 3.22 million persons in 2000 to 14.46 million in 2015, and private companies, 12.86 million to 111.80 million. As result of economic restructuring and opening up, China's non-public economy is growing. By 2013, the non-public economy had created 80 per cent of urban employment and 90 per cent of new job opportunities and had contributed 60 per cent of GDP and 69 per cent of tax revenue (press conference at the second session of the 12th national committee of the Chinese People's Political Consultative Conference (CPPCC), 6 March, 2014).

26. It was not until 1994 that the word 'unemployment' was officially used and recognized, instead of the previous wording 'waiting for a job', an expression which puts the unemployed directly under the umbrella of the socialist labour security system and hides the shame of unemployment as a social issue. It has been hard to change the system of lifetime guaranteed employment without making compromises. The central government's dogmatic policy used to require 'internal digestion as a rule, dismissal as an exception', which meant that the employer had to settle surplus labourers within enterprises or reallocate jobs as much as possible so as to ensure low redundancy and reduce social unrest.

In 1995, China determined to create 10 million jobs annually for urban labourers from the year of 1996 up until the year 2000.[10] A re-employment project was launched for redundant workers and the unemployed by adopting both policy support and employment service, giving full play to initiatives from government and enterprises, labourers and society; combining enterprise employment, self-employment and social support; and providing employment guidance for

8. Reuter News Service, 3 July 1996 China: China Private Business Booms Despite 'Squeeze'.
9. See Communique of the State Statistical Bureau of the PRC on Statistics for China, National Social-Economic Development in 1994, in Gazette of the State Council of the PRC, 8 March, Issue No. 4 (1995).
10. Wu Naitao, 'Government Adopts New Employment Strategy', in *Beijing Review*, 30 October– 5 November 1995 at p. 4.

unemployed and redundant workers.[11] It was officially revealed that the unemployment rate on record in urban areas was in the range of 3-4.3 per cent in the past two decades, with 4.3 per cent in 2009 as the highest.

In the prospect of China's 13th five-year plan (2016–2020), the targeted urban unemployment rate on record is to be held below 5 per cent, and 50 million new jobs will be created during the same period. Nationwide, the number of skill workers will be 170 million including one third of high skilled workers amounting to 55 million. China has provided around 13 million new jobs each year for the last four consecutive years since 2013. It is worth noticing that to realize the 13th five-year employment development plan, challenges and opportunities go hand in hand, in particular the challenge of securing employment while conducting supply-side structural reform, which would reduce redundancy in the sectors such as steel, coal, mining and other industries.

27. In the 1990s the process of establishing a labour market and a labour mobility policy has provided the possibility for millions of rural surplus labourers to sweep across China like water pouring through a broken dam. The Chinese term for such job-seekers from the countryside is 'floating populations', and the problem is comparable with issues of migration in some other developing countries. The key phrase of the previous flexible policy towards migrant workers was 'leaving farming land, but not the countryside'. The countryside surplus labourers have been encouraged by the state to stay in the countryside, and to engage in small industries, factories or small businesses so as to ease the pressures on the cities which can only provide jobs in construction or other 'bitter, tiring and dirty' work to these migrants. In the long term, the Chinese government will have to manage the 'floating populations' in a fair and orderly manner.

However, the 'three-world theory', invented by Mao Tse-Tung, can also apply to the vast territory of China with different labour requirements and labour conditions. From the west towards the coastal cities in the east, one may roughly divide China into three categories, i.e. less developed lands (third world), developing lands (second world) and developed lands (first world). It is a plain fact that the rural surplus labourers from less developed lands are pouring down to the developing lands (in the middle of China) and/or the developed land (in the coastal cities) whenever and wherever there are jobs of whatever kind. Inequality between rural migrant workers and urban residents is largely due to the unbalanced economic conditions from region to region. Rural migrant workers were believed to had reached to 120 million by 2006 according to various sources especially the Sectoral Recommendation for Solving the Problems of the Rural Workers issued by the State Council in January 2006 as well as the Investigation Report on Chinese Rural Migrant Workers, prepared by the Research Office of the State Council published in April 2006. In 2009 the floating populations (most of which are workers) amounted to 211 million, with average age of 27.3 years old; the numbers were increased to 236 million (Report on Development of Floating Population, by the former National Health and Family Planning Commission, 10 September 2013) and 247 million in 2012 and

11. Li Baoyong (the then Minister of Labour), 'China to Re-Employ Eight Millon Over Five Years', in *Beijing Review*, 30 October–5 November, 1995 at p. 8.

2015 respectively (2015 Statistical Bulletin of the National Economic and Social Development, PRC, by News Agency, 1 March 2016). No country in the world could painfully but peacefully deal with such enormous unprecedented mobility of peoples and working forces. The hardship of migrant workers has finally touched the hearts of the legislator and society at large to improve social justice by extending the boundary of equality under the umbrella of the labour law to cover such rural migrant workers. It is found that in hiring rural migrant workers, employers incline to circumvent and/or violate of existing labour norms for the sake of labour costs, while the enforcement institution at various levels is seeking a balance between economic development and protection of the interests of the employees. Rural migrant workers, who often work under the cover of certain subcontractor arrangements, are helping themselves in a variety of collective ways.

§6. Fundamental Political, Social and Cultural Values

28. The basic concept in social and political ideology is solidarity and stability. Individuals, society and the state are never regarded as being separate or independent from each other. Workers' solidarity under state paternalism is achieved through the political ethic of three levels of obedience, i.e. individuals obey the collective, the subordinate obeys the superior and locals obey the central government. The final application of these 'three obediences' in political life is that the whole CPC must obey its central committee.

29. Adherence to an officially recognized doctrine is required. Marxism-Leninism and Mao Tse-Tung's thought is still theoretically to be followed. But, on the other hand, traditional humanism, tolerance and the direct moral consequence of virtue and vice are commonly accepted in daily life. Indeed, Chinese society is used to living with the double value system, i.e. an official one and the one prevailing among the common people.

30. The relationship and interdependence between rights and duties are emphasized. It is proclaimed that every citizen enjoys the rights and at the same time must perform the duties prescribed by the Constitution and the law (see Art. 33 of the Constitution). The linkage of individual rights to the performance of social duties is reinforced both by Marxist teachings and by the Chinese philosophy of obedience. Under both teachings the exercise of citizens' rights and freedoms may not infringe upon the interests of the state, of society and of the collective or upon the lawful freedoms and rights of other citizens. Constitutional rights go beyond individualism; collectivism rather than individualism is the presumption for the constitutional protection of citizens' social, economic and cultural rights. Work and receiving an education are provided for in the Constitution as a right and a duty of citizens simultaneously.

31. Socialist democracy is deemed to be at a higher level than the democracy of capitalist countries. However, the fulfilment of democracy is believed to be limited to the level of social, economic and cultural development. China proclaims that it is at the primary stage of socialist development, therefore, human rights protection and political freedom are substantially restricted to that level of development. Presumably, the highest development level is the so-called high developed socialist state with a highly developed material civilization and spiritual civilization in which a sound socialist democracy would be possible.

32. Sound socialist legal systems will be developed corresponding to the development of a sound socialist democracy. The legal system is traditionally and is still, to a great extent, considered as a tool of the state, a monitor and controller of the society, a systematic force by which order can be maintained. Nevertheless, the doctrine of the rule of law is being more and more accepted and established, while government functions, including the judicial function, and their exercise are subject to constitutional limitation and regulated by administrative law. The consciousness of citizenship is becoming a topic rather than a constitutional state, due to, amongst other things, the lack of a certain profound background to develop a judicial supervisory mechanism to guard the supremacy of the Constitution.

33. Work is considered as a matter of honour for every citizen who is able to work. The socialist work ethic is advocated by the Constitution and the law, under which work is not only the right but also the duty of the citizen. It is a socialist principle that wealth distribution must be in accordance with the work contribution. The Constitution provides that the state shall create conditions for employment, enhancing occupational safety and health, improving working conditions and, on the basis of expanded production, increasing remuneration for work and welfare benefits (Art. 42). A new type of market-oriented employment mechanism is still in the process of being established. Contractual work relations have been introduced into the employment system whereby a worker's honour is somehow measured against the market forces. Culturally, labour remains a fundamental value in society and it is believed that prosperity can be achieved only through hard work. The mixture of market orientated labour reform and the traditional work ethic to some extent links formal labour legislation with informal practice.

34. Private property and the individual economy are recognized by the existing Constitution and the reform policy. Fair competition in areas of economic activity has been introduced by legislation and enforced by the market regulation mechanism, resulting in more and more social consciousness of equality, fairness and prosperity.

35. 'The Golden Way' refers to the common knowledge of living and the principle of a realistic attitude, in which neither the extremist, nor the rationalist way is conceived as being right. The idea of reaching compromises is to make an effort to find the way to achieve or prolong harmony. Therefore, neither conflict nor surrender is the approach. This philosophy directly and indirectly has implications for labour relationship and social norms in China. To balance the uneven changes taking place in China, the key words which have been adopted by the Chinese government since 1990 are 'reform, development and stability'. At the beginning of the 21st century, the Chinese authorities were seeking to mould popular opinion and thought by calling for the building up of a well-off society in which harmony is an essential requirement among the social components. The 'Well-off and Harmonious Society' programme coincides with the traditional idea of a Confucian social blueprint mixed with Buddhist understandings of social norms. An environmentally friendly approach was recently added to the blueprint to highlight the moral quality of building the Chinese dream.

Chapter 2. Definitions and Concepts

§1. Labour Law as a Branch of the Legal System

36. As an independent branch of law in the Chinese legal system, labour law is referred to as the total of all legal norms which regulate labour relations. It includes the Labour Act and other labour statues, administrative labour law and regulations, local labour administrative laws and regulations and other normative documents and judicial interpretations. Labour law in its narrow sense is referred to as the Labour Act itself. Chinese jurisprudence sees labour law, like any other law, as norms of conduct which reflect the state will, are formulated by and with the consent of the state and enforced by state power. As a branch of the legal system, labour law has its specific regulated object, i.e. direct and indirect labour relations. Labour law's basic principles and doctrines which deal with labour relations cannot be replaced by other branches of the legal system. The labour issue is regarded as fundamental in a socialist country. Therefore, labour law occupies a very important position in the legal system.

37. Labour relations mean a kind of social relations arising from the recruitment, disposal, exchange, use, service, management and supervision of the labour force. Direct labour relations are defined as the relations directly between the employing unit and the employee in employment, the disposal and use of labour. The distinctive feature of the labour relation is that the employee economically, personally and legally is subordinate to the employing unit. The worker is at the employing unit's disposal, but is in a position which ought to receive special legal protection. Direct labour relations are formed on the basis of the rights and obligations between the employing unit and employee when they enter employment relations, during employment and on termination of employment relations. They include issues of labour contractual relations, working conditions, remuneration, discipline and collective agreements, etc.

Labour law also regulates indirect labour relations, which are defined as social relations closely connected to direct labour relations. These are providing service to, management and regulation of, and supervision over direct labour relations. They could be the pre-conditions for the formation of labour relations or as a direct consequence of them or could accompany the formation, modification and termination of labour relations. Numerous indirect labour relations exist in state labour management, the employment service, the administration of the social insurance agency, labour dispute settlement, labour supervision, etc. It must be noted that the distinction between direct and indirect labour relations by analysis does not imply that there is a hierarchical relationship between the two. In addition, the difference between the two labour relations has no effect on their degree of importance. Labour law focuses on both categories of labour relations, which are differentiated from other social relations.

38. The 1994 Labour Act provides the legal basis for normative forces of collective agreement and individual labour contracts. Some terms in individual labour contracts regarding working conditions, minimum wages and other matters are bound by collective agreement, if any. Both collective agreements and individual labour contracts are obliged to comply with minimum standards established by provisions in the Labour Act. The standards set forth in the collective agreements shall prevail, if they are more favourable to employees. These indicate that the particular method of legal regulation in Chinese labour law is somewhat different from that of other branches of law. Since China has been developing its labour law in the market economy setting, minimum standards in wages, working hours and other spheres of labour law have been established so that labour relations apply fair rules with a compulsory minimum.

In dealing with labour relations, a tripartite participation has been to some extent introduced into labour law, though the practice of tripartite participation has not progressed much in over 30 years since 1994. The method and the concept is playing its role in adjusting labour relations. Nevertheless, it is still the case that free room for the parties to the individual labour contract and collective agreement is provided only to the extent that law and policy allow.

39. The subject of labour relations is covered by different legislation and regulations. State public servants and peasants are not within the scope of regulations in the Labour Act. Only those employees who have contractual labour relations with state agencies, institutional organizations and social groups are within the scope of the application of the Labour Act.[12] Those who work in state agencies, institutional organizations and social groups with which no labour contractual relationships is established are not subject to the Labour Act. Those enterprises, individual economic organizations inside the People's Republic of China (the employing unit) and employees who have labour relations with the employing unit will, however, fall within the ambit of the Act.[13] The Chinese Labour Act refers to workers or labourers not as white-collar workers and blue-collar workers. It is the intent of the Labour Act to minimize the differences between the so-called 'mass', i.e. the normal worker, and enterprise cadres, i.e. managerial, technical or political bureaucrats in enterprises under the previous planned economy in China.

§2. Delimitation of Labour Law from Other Branches of Law

40. In some aspects of contractual relationships, civil law and labour law may have similarities, but fundamental differences can be found with respect to regulated objects and the status of the subjects under the two branches of law. Labour relations governed by labour law are not independent from the employing unit, and while the work contractual relationship under civil law may be independent from the occupation, specific work is covered by a specific contract. The status of subjects (natural persons and legal persons) in a civil legal relationship is one of equality and independence, while in labour legal relations the parties thereto are

12. See Article 2 of the Labour Act in the *International Encyclopaedia for Labour Law and Industrial Relations* (Legislation) PR China, p. 101.
13. *Ibid.*

subordinated. However, labour law does not exclude the possible application of civil law in relation to sanctions imposed on violation of the legal interests and rights of workers. For example, Article 105 of the Labour Act stipulates that where there are provisions of laws or administrative regulations on the punishment of violations of legal rights and interests of workers as stipulated by the Labour Act, such provisions shall apply.

41. In China, labour law has a close relationship with economic law. Economic law is defined as the legal norm to regulate economic relations arising from the administration of the national economy and economic activities of various economic organizations. Economic law has played and is still playing an important role in numerous economic relationships, including employment planning, established under the state plan. Economic law is used to organize and manage the economy by legal means, while safeguarding the state macro-control over the national economy. Its rule sometimes overlaps with the labour law with respect to the indirect labour relations. However, the function of labour law is based on the workers' point of view and is to protect the legitimate rights and interests of workers from being violated. In addition, the subjects of economic legal relations regulated by economic law are mainly between legal persons, while labour legal relations are between individual workers and employing units.

The recent development of labour law in China shows a trend that it is becoming more and more independent and separate from economic law and administrative law, both of which once had dominant positions in regulating labour issues in a planned economy, including employment planning, wages and labour insurance, etc.

42. The differences between labour law and social security law are quite a recent topic in Chinese legislation and jurisprudence. The socialist labour security system was governed by labour administration regulations or, essentially, by administrative law. It was the socialist assumption that social security should be promoted by production and fulfilled in the state employer–workers forum, rather than by a protective policy of income redistribution at the social level. As labour law once also overemphasized its functions in increasing labour productivity, improving efficiency and workers' welfare under the state plan, labour law and social security regulations were thus ideologically interrelated.

Social security legislation is being developed, since the Labour Act provided the clear legal framework in its Chapter 9 entitled 'Social Insurance and Welfare'. The Labour Act in fact summed up the development of social security reform, as part of market-oriented labour reform, since the middle of the 1980s. Under the reform experiment, independent social security funds have been established and administered by independent institutions. Numerous regulations have been introduced transforming, consciously and unconsciously, social security regulation from a paternalistic nature to a social nature. Social security law as an independent branch of law is being formed to establish social safety nets covering the insured, not just workers, and providing criteria for entitlement to the necessary social benefits, including social insurance, social relief, social welfare, military care, housing benefit, etc., while labour law focuses on the protection of workers' rights and interests arising from labour relations, which should not be equal to or even replace social safety nets.

43. Chinese jurisprudence holds that the distinctive method of regulation of labour law differs from other branches of law, especially civil law, administrative law and social security law. Labour law regulates labour relations neither by means of coercive administrative, as adopted by administrative law, nor by means of free will and equality between the parties as adopted by the civil law or through the state obligatory regulated legal method as adopted by social security law. As stated above, labour law combines various regulations by means of individual labour contracts, collective agreement and legislative regulations. The comprehensive regulation of labour law also encourages a genuine consultation mechanism to further develop between the social partners in China.

Chapter 3. The Historical Background

§1. Brief History of Labour Legislation before 1949

44. During the imperial period, Chinese labourers experienced a long history of struggle in order to change their position as slaves in the agricultural society, for their subsistence. Dynasties were frequently overthrown and replaced by one after another, but the situation changed little for the labourer. At the beginning of the 20th century, the industrial workers emerged as a new dynamic force in modern Chinese history. According to Mao Tse-Tung's class analysis, the severity and cruelties of the oppression suffered by the Chinese labourers were very rarely found among the various other nations in the world, because the Chinese labourers were subject to a threefold oppression by imperialism, the bourgeoisie and feudal forces.[14] Labour law developments can be seen as part of the modern history in which the Chinese labourers struggled to their deaths for their economic, social and political positions.

45. The brief history from the beginning of the century can be illustrated in three parts under different political regimes. The first part is the so-called period of the Peking warlord government lasting from the Republican Revolution of 1911 until 1927. During that period, earlier developments of trade union and labour legislation focused on the very basic demand of workers for legal protection. The first congress of labour organizations held in 1922 passed a proposal for an eight-hour working-day. An outline of the labour legislation was drafted with 19 articles, which was never accepted by the Peking Parliament.

46. The second part is Canton's revolutionary government and the Nanking Nationalist government which lasted until 1949 and followed along the lines of Dr Sun Yan-Sen's republican politics. The Canton revolutionary government made an effort to develop labour laws especially with respect to union rights. The trade union regulations, promoted in November 1924, recognized the right to organize trade unions and the right to strike. However, on 12 April 1927, Dr Sun's successor Chiang Kai-Shek had those trade unionists and strikers under the leader of the Communist Party in Shanghai massacred and took power with his Nationalist Party forming the government. From that time two parallel legislative systems were developed, i.e. the legislation of the Nationalist government and the legislation which the Communist Party applied in areas where its military forces had control.

From 1927 to 1949 the Nanking Nationalist government published many labour regulations concerning labour contract law, collective agreements, trade union law, factory law, labour dispute law, etc. However, the labour legislation under the Nanking nationalist government made little change to work conditions and working positions, partly because they were too restrictive and impractical. Employers only referred to this labour legislation when it suited their own needs, for example, the prohibition of strikes. The poor economic conditions, dictated politics and war prevented the workers from asserting their rights. However, the bloody struggle of the

14. See *Selected Mao Tse-Tung Works* 1952 edn., Vol. 2, at p. 639.

working class had strengthened its self-consciousness. In alliance with the peasants, the working class fought for political power, instead of seeking to have its rights protected passively.

47. The third part is the Jiangxi Republic of Chinese Soviets lasting from 1930 to 1937 and the Yanan regimes from 1937 to 1949. The Jiangxi Republic of Chinese Soviets successfully adopted the Labour Protection Law in 1930, which contains eight chapters, including:

- scope of the application;
- contract of employment;
- working hours;
- rest time;
- wages;
- protection of women and minors;
- trade unions; and
- social security and welfare.

In 1931 the Labour Law of the Chinese Soviets was adopted and came into effect on 1 January 1932, but it was found that the standards which it set were too high to be implemented in armed controlled areas which were in a very difficult economic situation. The new Labour Law was promulgated on 15 October 1933 with 15 chapters and 121 articles replacing the previous 1931 labour law of the Chinese Soviets. However, its implementation was very limited due to the reality not being comparable to the approach of the labour law.

The Yanan government enacted the Provisional Regulations on Labour Protection on 1 November 1941 with two amendments in 1942 and 1943. It contains seven chapters and 45 articles covering wages, rest time, labour protection, labour contracts and employees. Most of the provisions were reasonable under the special conditions at that time; working hours were stipulated as ten in principle, and working time for miners not to exceed nine hours. The employer was also prohibited from beating, torturing and insulting employees or adopting other means of exploitation. In summary, the experience of labour legislation adopted by the Communist government in its occupied regions demonstrated fundamental labour law principles and practice which served as the historical origin for the legislation in the 1950s after the establishment of the People's Republic of China.

§2. Brief History of Labour Legislation after 1949

48. Before the declaration of the founding of the People's Republic of China in October 1949, all existing legislation and legal systems under the Nationalist government were declared to be abolished in accordance with the Instructions on Abolishing the Collection of the Six Laws of the Nationalist Party and the Confirmation of the Judicial Principles of the Liberated Areas. The Common Programme adopted by the Chinese People's Political Consultative Conference in September 1949, which served as a temporary Constitution until the 1954 Constitution, confirmed the breakdown of the old social system, including the established legal order, while establishing a new revolutionary social and legal order. This approach to the legal system and legislation is based on the Marxist doctrine of destroying the bourgeois state machine, including the legal system, and replacing it with the new proletarian dictatorship and socialist legal system. The new socialist state is believed to be one which itself will naturally demolish the state and law as an institutionalized alien.

49. Before and after the 1954 Constitution, China went through radical changes to establish socialist economic, political and social systems using Stalin's Soviet system as the first reference. Legal institutions and legal philosophy, copied largely from Russia, served well for this purpose.

The old labour practice under the Nationalist government and particularly the physical searching for textile workers was abolished in 1950. Measures were taken against the so-called 'recruiter' system in goods transportation, and the 'foreman' system in the coal mines. The earlier 1950s' policy was to use, limit and reform the capitalist industrial and commercial establishment before the nationwide nationalization of private industrial and commercial enterprises took place in the mid-1950s. Numerous labour regulations sought mainly to protect the interests of the employees who still worked under the contract system. Bargaining power had been enhanced. Employers' management powers of dismissal, workmen's compensation and labour safety had been reduced. Procedures for labour dispute settlements had been regulated.

By 1956, the ownership of all major enterprises had been declared as being brought under the control of the state and collectives. The contract system, with a few exceptions, was abolished, while the state took responsibility for recruiting employees through assignment by local labour bureaux according to state planning. A lifelong employment system was implemented, and all necessary social benefits, including housing, medical insurance, and pensions were provided by the state-owned or collectively owned enterprises. Private ownership and the private economy were reduced to a minimum. The immobility of the labour force was substantially limited, due to the close link between enterprises and social welfare under the public ownership system of the means of production. In this context, labour law after 1956 mainly focused on maintaining safe working conditions, labour insurance, and certifying standards for labour assignment. The basic labour systems and the majority policy formed in the 1950s and styled along old Soviet system lines changed little in the 1960s and 1970s.

50. Major legislation in the 1950s was as follows: the 1950 Trade Union Law, enacted by the Central People's government; the 1951 Labour Insurance Regulations (with amendments in 1953); Provisions regarding labour issues stipulated in the 1954 Constitution (Arts. 16, 19, 92, 93 and Art. 100); and Decisions on Wage Reform, promulgated by the State Council in 1956. Three industrial safety regulations were also enacted in 1956, namely, the Factory Safety and Hygiene Regulations; the Construction Instalment Project Safety Technique Regulations; and the Regulations on Reporting Injury and Casualties of Employees and Staff. China started drafting its first Labour Act in 1956, after the founding of the People's Republic of China. The draft work was forced to halt in 1957 when the 'campaign against rightists' turned down all efforts at legislation. Institutionalizing the legal system and legitimizing individual rights and interests were regarded as a 'Bourgeoise Right' movement which was deemed to be part of a revolt against communist ideology and the Communist Party's leadership.

51. In order to turn the communist ideology into reality, the so-called Great Leap Forward towards a communist society programme was launched in 1958. In rural areas, the commune system had been practised and in some areas the principle of the distribution of food and property according to one's needs had been exercised not long before hunger and national economic crisis spread all over the country at the beginning of the 1960s. Subsequent economic adjustment was made and chaos in labour administration was brought to order before another wave of chaos pushed the order away in 1966.

52. During the Great Cultural Revolution period from 1966 to 1976, there was in general very little labour legislation enacted. Mao's quotations and the party's policy functioned as law or replaced the provisions of the law. Workers' initial enthusiasm about their revolutionary rights and initiatives in the earlier years of the Cultural Revolution were led and misled by the party line. The result was that law and the legal order were either ignored or only regarded as an enforcement tool to fulfil the state plan or party's policy. For example, with respect to wage planning, the State Council issued a Notice Regarding Adjustment to the Wages of Some Workers and Staff in 1971. In 1975 the State Council issued a Notice Regarding the Issuing of the Protocols of the National Safety Production Meeting, which called for greater worker discipline and labour safety.

At the enterprise level the party line and the state plan directives were carried out by the collective managerial body, the so-called 'revolutionary committee' of enterprises, institutions and social organizations. Most previous managers, educated engineers, technicians and other professionals were forced to 'reform mind through manual labour'. Young graduates were allocated jobs 'up to the mountains, down to the countryside'. During those ten years, the massive class struggle constantly affected the normal production order.

§3. Labour Legislation from 1978 to 1995 and Beyond

53. The Great Cultural Revolution was officially declared to be at an end at the 11th General Meeting of the Communist Party in August 1977. Subsequently, the social and legal system were gradually restored. Production activity was regarded as being of primary importance, instead of political campaigning.

Meanwhile, emphasis was placed on the education system and science development in the drive towards modernization. Labour discipline was enhanced, and the 'Revolutionary Committee' as the management organ in enterprises was replaced by the manager responsibility system. In October 1978, the trade unions held their Ninth National Congress.

54. The third session of the 11th General Meeting of the Communist Party of China held in December 1978 was believed to have marked significant policy changes in economic, social and legal aspects. Following this, a liberalized economic policy was adopted, and enterprise reform directly touched upon management and labour issues. In the 1980s, the Chinese government launched an experimental reform in employment systems in state enterprises by using the contract form to recruit new workers. The initial idea was to establish a certain degree of mobility in the labour force. The early experiment was carried out in the special economic zones and several other provinces. On 22 February 1983 the Ministry of Labour and Personnel issued a notice calling on enterprises to actively experiment with the contract labour system. Meanwhile, the Provisional Regulations on Examinations of Workers' Technique were adopted in order to regulate new employees according to their merits and qualifications. The contract labour system, in competing with permanent state workers, had brought about ideological justifications in the socialist labour system. Dual employment systems were developed, i.e. one based on contractual employment relationships and one based on the state assignment employment system. On 12 July 1986 the State Council issued four sets of regulations regarding contract employment and providing standards for recruitment, termination of contracts and unemployment and other benefits. These four regulations are known as the Provisional Regulations on the Implementation for the Contract System in State-Owned Enterprises; the Provisional Regulation on the Recruitment of Workers by State Owned Enterprises; the Provisional Regulations on Dismissal of Employees of State Owned Enterprises in Violation of Discipline; and the Provisional Regulations on Unemployment Insurance for Employees of State Owned Enterprises.

55. The second reform introduced since 1978 was the democratic management system along with enterprise reform. The workers' congress was restored after 1978. The system had been introduced in 1957 but was abolished shortly thereafter. In 1981, the Provisional Regulations on State Industrial Enterprise Workers' Congress was issued by the State Council and Central Committee of the Communist Party. The same matter was also regulated in 1986. The state enterprise reform also called for the separation of enterprise management from government administration. Enterprises were reformed so that they became independent legal persons, which took responsibility for their own losses and benefits, while management power was granted to managers. The Regulations on Factory Director of the Industrial Enterprises of 1986; the Bankruptcy Law (on a trial basis) of 1988; the Law of the PRC on Industrial Enterprises Owned by the Whole People of 1988 and the Regulations on Transforming the Management Mechanism of Enterprises of 1992 were sequential steps taken to encourage further reform in state enterprises in the 1990s. Regulations were also enacted at the end of the 1980s and the beginning of the 1990s governing collective and private enterprises. The Company Law of 1994 led to further enterprise reform which had a direct impact on individual labourers who experienced the process leading to the destruction of the so-called 'iron rice bowl' labour insurance system, and the inflexible wage system.

56. Numerous regulations were adopted with respect to labour discipline, wages, home leave, industry safety, labour inspection, employment service, insurance and welfare and other matters. Since 1984 various forms of the economic responsibility system were promoted to emphasize the distribution of income based on the contribution of work. They guided the 1984–85 wage reform in state enterprises, state agencies and institutions. In 1993 Regulations on Minimum Wage in Enterprises were adopted. More legislation has been enacted, for example the Labour Dispute Regulations (1987 and 1993), the Labour Protection of Female Workers Regulations (1988), the Prohibition from Using Child Labour Regulations (1991), the Temporary Workers Regulations (1989), the Labour Employment Services Enterprises Administrative Regulations (1990), the Mines Safety Act (1992), and the Trade Union Law (1992, and revised in 2001).

57. In order to handle the issues of redundant old workers and staff left over from the Cultural Revolution period, the Standing Committee of the National People's Congress in 1978 approved the State Council's two measures to organize the old, sick and handicapped cadres and retirement of workers. Meanwhile, dogmatic employment measures had been taken to solve the urban unemployment by allowing another member of the family to take the job of those workers who were entitled to retirement or early retirement.

58. Most significant provisions regarding labour issues were provided for in the 1982 Constitution. The constitutional basis for further labour legislation can be found in provisions on worker participation in management decision-making (Arts. 16 and 17), rights and duties of work, labour remuneration, working conditions, safety and labour protection, vocational training (Art. 42), right to rest (Art. 43), state labour and social policy, especially the right to receive material assistance (Arts. 42, 44 and 45). In addition, freedom of association (Art. 35), equality between men and women (Art. 48) and other civil rights provisions are also basic for the protection of workers' rights. Noticeably, the right to strike is not provided in the 1982 Constitution. The socialist commodity economy was the political economy theory for the pro-reform 1982 Constitution while China recognized that it was in the primary stage of socialist development. At the beginning of the 1990s, commodity theory, with its emphasis on guidance from state plan to the market was revised to 'socialist market economy' theory and contained in the 1993 and 1999 constitutional amendments. The constant revision of the state-endorsed theory, reflected in constitutional provisions, tends to support vigorous changes in the economy and legal policy in general, and labour policy and labour law in particular.

59. The drafting work of the Labour Act was restored in 1978 and thereafter, but encountered difficulty in formulating its scope of application, and determining the appropriate legal policy to match the unstable reform experiences which differed from region to region. However, after summarizing experiences from more than a decade's reform and under the guidance of the market oriented legal policy, adopted in the 1993 constitutional amendment, the Labour Act was finalized, with more than 30 drafts over 15 years. It was passed by the Standing Committee of the National Peoples Congress on 5 July 1994, effective as of 1 January 1995. It enshrined labour reform while providing the basic legal platform for further labour legislation in the late 1990s and for the 21st century. The Labour Act contains 107 articles with 13 chapters, i.e.:

Chapter 1 General provisions;
Chapter 2 Employment promotion;
Chapter 3 Labour contracts and collective agreements;
Chapter 4 Working hours, rest and vacations;
Chapter 5 Wages;
Chapter 6 Labour safety and health;
Chapter 7 Special protection for female workers and juvenile workers;
Chapter 8 Vocational training;
Chapter 9 Social insurance and welfare;
Chapter 10 Labour disputes;
Chapter 11 Supervision and inspection;
Chapter 12 Legal liability;
Chapter 13 Supplementary provisions.

Major achievements have been made in four aspects under the Labour Act. It ensures the individual labour contract system and establishes a collective agreement system; it shortens working hours and increases holidays; it further establishes a minimum wage system and constitutes a social insurance and welfare structure. The Labour Act intends to unify the legal treatment towards employees (including foreign workers employed in China) in different industrial sectors with different forms of ownership. In order to implement the Labour Act, nine single-item laws were drafted to cover almost all issues listed under each chapter of the Labour Act, i.e. the Employment Promotion Law; the Labour Contract Law; the Occupational Skill Development Law; the Wage Law; the Social Insurance Law; the Labour Protection Law; the Work Safety Law; the Production Safety Law; and the Labour Disputes Law. In 1996, the Vocational Education Law was promulgated. In 2001 the Occupational Disease Prevention Law was promulgated (with further amendments made in 2011, 2016 and 2017). In 2002 the Production Safety Law was promulgated. In 2007, Law on Mediation and Arbitration of Labour Disputes was promulgated. In 2007, the Labour Contract Law was promulgated which was amended in 2012 limiting the use of 'dispatched labourers' and laying down explicit rules that dispatched laborers are entitled to the same rights as 'regular contract employees'. Further, the Provisional Rules on Labour Dispatch was released by the Ministry of Human Resource and Social Security in 2013 in order to consolidate labour dispatch administration. In 2010, the Social Insurance Law was promulgated. The Social Insurance Law regulates comprehensively and systematically basic pension, medical, work-related injury, maternity and unemployment insurance and explicitly lays down the rules for the collection, handling, supervision of the social insurance administration and related liabilities.

Seventeen administrative regulations were enacted by the then Ministry of Labour (which was later restructured as the Ministry of Labour and Social Security, then further renamed as the Ministry of Human Resource and Social Security) to accompany the Labour Act, and local labour administrations have been requested to implement them thoroughly and to put in place local regulations and rules linking up with the actual situation in the locale. The 17 sets of regulations are as follows:

1. Notice concerning the Implementation of the System for the Guaranteed Minimum Wage;
2. Measures on Occupational Guidance;
3. Measures on Administration of Labour Inspection Personnel;
4. Provisions on the Enterprise Personnel Reduction of an Economic Nature;
5. Provisional Regulations regarding the Administration of Employment of the Migrant Agricultural Labour Force Across Provinces;
6. Regulations on Medical Leave for Enterprise Workers and Staff who are Sick or Have Non-work Related Injuries;
7. Measures on Economic Compensation for Violation or Cancellation of Labour Contracts;
8. Regulations on Collective Agreements;
9. Provisional Regulations on Payment of Wages;
10. Regulations on Occupational Training;
11. Regulations on the Special Protection of Juvenile Workers;
12. Measures on the Approval of Enterprise Implementation of Systems of Non-fixed Period and Overall Calculation of Work Times;
13. Regulations on the Substantive Supervision of Occupational Training;
14. Administrative Measures for Mining Safety Inspection Personnel;
15. Implementing Measures for Inspection of Safety in the Mining, Construction Works;
16. Provisional Measures on Maternity Insurance for Enterprise Workers and Staff; and
17. Measures on Punishment for the Violation of Labour Law.

In addition, the Regulations on Labour Security and Supervision (promulgated in 2004), Rules on Service and Administration of Employment (promulgated in 2007 and amended in 2015), Regulations on Paid Annual Leave of Employees (promulgated in December 2007 and taking effect in January 2008) and the Implementing Rules on Labour Contract Law (promulgated in 2008) set out the further implementation of the statutory labour norms in judicial and administrative practice. Significantly, the Employment Promotion Law (promulgated in 2007 and amended in 2015), the Labour Contract Law (promulgated in 2007 and amended in 2012) and the Law on Mediation and Arbitration of Labour Disputes (promulgated in December 2007 and taking effect in May 2008) provide the advanced 'legal GPS' to guide the 'driving behaviour' of the employers and employees in the labour market.

60. The brief history of labour legislation from 1978 up to 2018 could be divided into three stages, namely, from 1978 until 1995 as the initial legislation foundation period; from 1995 up to 2008 as the legal advance period; and from 2008 through

2018 as the labour right's enhancement period. Four essentials of Chinese labour legislation development are observed and found by the author as follows:

(a) a stable and sustainable legal ecology has been shaped under the Labour Act with its accompanying regulations compatible with Chinese political, economic and cultural changes over the last four decades. The further development of labour legislation and legal policy after year 1995 has helped to change the pattern and the nature of labour relations in China from paternalism into market self-regulation. From perspective of social jurisprudence, the creation and working of labour law in China are in some way reliant on the gradual privatization of the state economy and liberalization of social life, especially systematic implementation of the family planning policy, introduced in 1973 and further restrictively implemented in the one-child policy in 1980s, 1990s and 2000s, which strikingly satisfied a nationwide collective consciousness of the necessity for reduction of self-reproduction of the labour army. Chinese labourers are taught to acquire a quality of life by more self-initiative in earning and less reliance on having children. However, it recently been discovered that the new generation of labourers will not be able to satisfy the demand for financing the ageing society. The lifting of the one-child policy in 2016 will eventually increase the numbers of the labour forces along with the developed labour norms in favour of future growth;

(b) improvement and integration of labour standards are facilitating the change of politics and ideology. The constant modification of understanding of Marxist teachings mainly served the needs of state policy shift while dogmatic labour regulations were functioning as cautious measures to smooth the process of the transition from a state-planned to a market-oriented labour administration, especially during the legal advance period (1995–2008) during which the fundamental quest for labour standards was to maintain the social harmony. Anti-discrimination in employment was and is still not fully regulated. Chinese modernization gave priority to protection of property rights and civil rights in a broad sense;

(c) the emphasis on the individual labour contract by Chinese labour law is intended not only to ensure the employers' autonomy in employment of personnel, but also the individual's right to work of his choosing. In addition, the collective consultation and agreement system is adopted to protect the collective right, exercised at a local level within limited industrial sectors in which neither independent unions, nor labour NGOs are evolved with bargaining powers in a collective consultation mechanism. Consequently, binary labour contract protection is rather thin. The justiciability for labour dispute cases under the individual labour contract is rather broad;

(d) from a global economic point of view, the dialogues with industrialized nations partially contribute to the shaping of Chinese industrial policy and labour legislation, while China's economy joins in the globalization process. The development of Chinese labour legislation has evidenced the impact of foreign capital inflow as one of the driving forces for improving the compatibility of the Chinese system with the criteria (including the international labour standards) recognized by the international community. Such dialogues have a great impact on upgrading Chinese labour-related standards and increasing awareness of social responsibilities for the employers (e.g. rest and working hours, minimum wage system, the labour contract system, respect for intellectual property and protection of the environment, etc.). Nevertheless, Chinese labour law pursues perfection, while building up its own jurisprudence foundation.

Chapter 4. Role of the Government and the Social Partners in the Shaping and Administration of Labour Law and Industrial Relations

§1. The Government's Role in Legislation and Industrial Relations

61. The Chinese legal and political situation indicates that the state is acting as a monitor as well as an umbrella in protecting labourers. The government is implementing a social strategy which is always a reflection of the orientation of the social blueprints. The awakening of Chinese traditional values in governance is part of the cultural pride acquired during the last three decades when the political and economic environment provided a certain degree of flexibility and certain options for building up a civil society in which the rule of law is the fundamental value. In terms of labour administration, Article 9 of the Labour Act stipulates the division of responsibility of the labour administration at central and local level. Governmental supervisory and management work lies largely within the labour administrative department. However, for the purpose of specific statutory legislation, authorized local departments and other relevant departments usually conduct investigation and research, solicit opinions directly from different interest groups, and summarize and report to the central government. At central government level, the Ministry of Human Resource and Social Security and the Legal Affairs Bureau of the State Council normally cooperate to draft the proposed legislation, and where necessary, directly conduct field investigation and research by themselves in the selected location. After the proposed statutory legislation has been submitted by the State Council to the National People's Congress or its standing committee, the latter may, before deliberation and discussion on the proposed legislation, widely solicit opinions on the legislation from employers or employers' organizations and workers' representatives or the employees' organization. As for administrative regulations, either the State Council or the Ministry of Human Resource and Social Security may draft the regulations which fall within their own authority. Local government at provincial level may enact implementation rules concerning the particular issues of labour in accordance with law and national regulations, in line with local conditions.

62. The government's role in relation to industrial relations can be seen in its labour and social policy, especially its employment policy, job security and wage policy. Its efforts towards the promotion of employment by regulation of the labour market, implementation of employment and re-employment schemes, etc., are very crucial to stabilizing the social unrest resulting from economic restructuring and the laying-off of surplus workers. For the purpose of job security, the central government's dogmatic policy requires that the employer resettles surplus workers within the enterprise or reallocates jobs as far as possible so as to secure employment for them. Employees therefore do not become officially registered as unemployed in society. Instead they are paid basic wages until they find another job within or outside the enterprise. To relieve the tensions between the government and the rural migrant workers, several major administrative regulations concerning rural migrant workers, promulgated in 2003, 2004 and 2006, have made the following efforts to improve conditions for rural migrant workers. These regulations permit the mobility of labour from the rural areas and waive the approval procedures for migrant workers (according to the Notice on Improving the Labour Administration and Service to Rural Migrant Workers in the Cities 2003); call for the payment of overdue wages owed to migrant workers in the construction industry (according to the Interim Regulations on the Wage Payment for Migrant Workers in the Construction Industry 2004 September); and urge social security coverage and overall improvement in the social treatment of migrant workers (according to Several Recommendations for Solving the Problems of the Rural Workers Jan 2006 (Gufa 2006 no. 5). It should be noted that all such legal provisions are in the form of the administrative stipulations. Administrative stipulations are weaker than legislative statutes in terms of enforcement application, compliance for labour inspection and justiciability. It is the first time that the Chinese Labour Promotion Law (effective as of 1 January 2008) has called for 'fair employment', which is the Chinese understanding or interpretation of equality in employment. The Labour Promotion Law (Art. 31) calls for rural workers employed in cities to enjoy labour rights equal to those of urban workers; and no discriminatory restrictions may be applied to rural workers seeking employment in cities. The Labour Contract Law amended in 2012 also reiterates, among others, the principle of equal pay for equal work for dispatched workers including peasant workers dispatched through labour agents.

Furthermore, to materialize the transformation from planned economy to market economy, an obligatory insurance scheme has been introduced and supervised by the government to ease unemployment problems. The unemployment insurance funds were set up in 1986 to cope with the labour contract system and the implementation of the Bankruptcy Law. The funds were generated to cope with the 600,000 unemployed originally estimated from state enterprises each year. But during 1986–1990 only 200,000 benefited from the unemployment insurance. From 1988 to 1990 only one state enterprise became bankrupt. The Tianjin Bohai Beer Factory was the largest state enterprise to become bankrupt in 1994–1995, with 600 employees and retired staff.[15] Dismissal of employees and revocation of employment contracts were once rare and as a result, the funds were left with a good reserve and able to meet requirements for increased expenditure in the first half of the 1990s.[16] 1996 is the first year of the Ninth Five-Year-Plan (1996 to 2000). The registered unemployment rate in official statistics in the past three decades was in range of 3–4 per cent and it has hovered at 4 per cent on average in the recent five years, around 9 million people. The Outline of the 13th Five-Year Plan of Ministry

15. See *People's Daily* overseas ed. 17 January 1995.
16. The *Beijing Review*, 30 October–5 November 1995 reported that according to the then Minister of Labour, in 1994 1.87 million people received unemployment benefits, a number equal to the total in the seven years since the unemployment insurance programme was launched.

of Human Resources and Social Security states that the registered urban unemployment rate will be held below 5 per cent in this period; more than 50 million new jobs will be created in cities and towns; participation in basic medical and pension insurance will cover 95 per cent of the target population in order to build a fairer and more sustainable social security system across China.

63. With regard to wage policy, the national labour authority exercises unified supervision over the national minimum wage system. In fixing a minimum wage, the local labour authority at provincial level is to work with the trade union and employer organization at the corresponding level, as required by the Regulations on Minimum Wages in Enterprises. The provincial minimum wage rate is endorsed by the national labour authority in consultation with the All-China Federation of Trade Unions (ACFTU) and the China Enterprise Directors' Association (CEDA)/ China Enterprises Association (CEA) under the same Regulations. Thus a tripartite system is practised with respect to minimum wage setting machinery. In August 2001, the Ministry of Labour and Social Security, ACFTU and China Enterprise Association (CEA) jointly established the State Tripartite Conference System of Labour Relation Coordination. In some provinces, a similar system has also been established. According to statistics of the Ministry of Human Resources and Social Security, from 2011 to 2015, the average annual increase rate was 13.1 per cent.

§2. Role of the Trade Union and Workers' Participation

64. Articles 5 to 7 of the 1992 Trade Union Law (as amended as 2001) provide for a triangular structural relationship between the trade unions, government and workers. Trade unions play dual roles in their relations to each of the other two social partners. In their relations with the government, they act as guardian of the collective interests of the workers, and at the same time, act as assistant to the government's work; in their relations with members of the union, they act as a protector for the workers as well as a superior who is to educate and mobilize them to work for the motherland as 'master of the state' so that the workers will accept government plans and policies.

65. Democratic management systems through employee participation in the decision-making process are carried out through the assembly of workers and the staff or workers congress in state and collective enterprises. According to the 1986 Regulations of Staff Sub-Congress in Industrial Enterprises Owned by the Whole People, the major functions and powers of the workers' congress are, amongst others, to discuss the report submitted by the factory director; to adopt the long-term business plan, wage and welfare plan proposed by the factory director. However, the workers' congress is required to follow the ideological and political leadership of the grassroots committees of the Communist Party in an enterprise. The trade union in the enterprise is the working organization of the workers' congress and oversees the day-to-day work of the workers' congress. The workers' congresses are called upon by the 1986 Regulations generally to actively support the factory director in exercising his authority in business and managerial decision-making. The Law of the PRC on Industrial Enterprises Owned by the Whole People of 1988 further stipulated the workers' right to participate in management. Article 8 of the Labour Act further developed the legal basis for workers' participation, in a sense of strengthening not only democratic management, but also the collective right to consultation (instead of the wording collective bargaining) with the employer. Democratic management system was exercised in state and collectively owned enterprises in the 1980s. With the development of law and practice, enterprises with all types of ownership systems are required to adopt company rules and regulations by the Assembly of Workers or the Staff Congress.

66. The recent development of corporate law, for example the Company Law of 1994, revised in 2005 (effective on 1 January 2006) and further revised in 2013 (effective on 1st March 2014), demonstrates that China has been adopting modern concepts of company management systems in which a company should seek advice from its trade union when discussing and deciding upon important issues on the restructuring or operation of the company (Arts. 17 and 18 of the Company Law). The members of the board of directors of a limited liability company invested in and established by two or more state-owned enterprises, or by two or more other state-owned investment entities shall include representatives of the staff and workers of that company (Art. 44 of the Company Law). In addition, Articles 51 and 117 of the Company Law require that a supervisory board, in a limited liability company with a relatively large-scale operation and in a company limited by shares, shall be established, and be composed of representatives of shareholders and an appropriate proportion of representatives of the company's staff and workers.

§3. The Employer's Role

67. The employer, as an independent legal entity, is subject to state macro-regulation, while it assumes its autonomous powers in recruitment, dismissal, wages and bonus and other matters within the scope stipulated by the laws. In the sector of state enterprises, the Law of the PRC on Industrial Enterprises Owned by the Whole People of 1988 and its implementing rules of 1992 (known as the Regulations on Transforming the Management Mechanism of the Industrial Enterprises Owned by the Whole People) confer more powers on employers in employment, management and operation of state enterprises, while ensuring, on the other hand, state supervision over and macro-regulation of state enterprises, by reducing direct state interference in the economic activities of enterprises. The process of separation of the state's right of ownership from the enterprise's right to operate resulted in the adjustment of the previously paternalistic relationship between government, state enterprises and employees. Employers are more independent from the government in their decision-making in matters regarding production and employment, etc., while the government assumes responsibilities for regulating the social and economic environment.

68. Employers play an important role in industrial relations in the context of the collective consultation. Article 8 of the Labour Act refers to the equal consultation between the assembly of employees or workers congress and the employer regarding protection of the legitimate rights and interests of employees. Although the terminology of collective bargaining, or collective negotiations, is not explicitly used either in the Trade Union Law or in the Labour Act, the Trade Union Law recognizes the practice of collective agreements (Art. 20). In Chinese 'collective consultation' is a more friendly and compromising way of saying 'negotiations'. In state undertakings, employers or employers' organizations are unlikely to take a position confronting the employees. They also take a cooperative position, in most cases, with the government towards the issues of industrial relations. The Labour Contract Law confirmed that a collective agreement should be entered into by the trade union and employer, and should be submitted to the labour administration authority. The collective agreement will become effective upon the lapse of 15 days beginning from the date of the receipt by the labour administration authority, if the authority does not raise any objections to it.

Chapter 5. Sources of Labour Law

§1. International Treaties

69. There is no constitutional approach to the supremacy of international law nor are there constitutionally established procedures for integrating international law into Chinese law.

70. In the 1990 Law of the PRC on the Procedure of the Conclusion of Treaties, there are no provisions on whether or not an international treaty to which China is a party should be given preference over domestic law. However, under general legal practice and some legislation, for example the 1986 General Principle of Civil Law (as amended in 2009), the 1989 Administrative Litigation Law, and the 1991 Civil Procedure Law, the binding force of international treaties which China has concluded or has acceded to is recognized; if there is a conflict between domestic law and an international treaty (except those provisions about which China has expressly made reservations) the treaty will prevail.

71. As far as international laws are concerned, United Nations' human rights conventions are of importance to Chinese labour law in general. In 1971 China resumed its membership of the United Nations, replacing the Taiwan Nationalist authorities, and since 1980 the Chinese government has ratified the following seven United Nations human rights conventions: the Convention on the Prevention and Punishment of the Crime of Genocide; the International Convention on the Suppression and Punishment of the Crime of Apartheid; the Convention on the Elimination of All Forms of Discrimination against Women; the International Convention on the Elimination of all Forms of Racial Discrimination; the Convention Relating to the Status of Refugees; the Protocol Relating to the Status of Refugees; the Convention against Torture and other Cruel, Inhuman or Degrading Treatment or Punishment.

72. On 28 February 2001 China ratified the International Covenant on Economic, Social and Cultural Rights. It is a step forward for China to pronounce on fundamental rights and their underlying values. China sees itself as in a position to influence the common destiny of humanity in which the development of such rights would be occur via global trade. The archaeological concept of the Silk Road has been activated, preparing for Chinese workers and capital to echo the roar of the awakening lion.

73. China was one of the founding states of the International Labour Organization (ILO). The Nationalist government in 1930 ratified 14 international labour conventions, and in 1944 China became a permanent member of the governing body of the ILO. In 1971 the governing body of the ILO passed a resolution to restore the People's Republic of China's membership status of the ILO in accordance with United Nations General Assembly Resolution No. 396V. The Chinese government did not participate formally in the activities of the ILO until 1983 at the 69th Session of the International Labour Conference when it resumed its position as a permanent member of the governing body of the ILO. In 1985 the Standing Committee of the National People's Congress recognized the 14 international labour conventions which the Nationalist government had ratified, namely the Convention Fixing the Minimum Age for Admission of Children to Employment at Sea 1920 (No. 7); the Convention Concerning the Rights of Association and Combination of Agricultural Workers 1921 (No. 11); the Convention Concerning the Application of Weekly Rest in Industrial Undertakings 1921 (No. 14); the Convention Fixing the Minimum Age for the Admission of Young People to Employment as Trimmers or Stokers 1921 (No. 15); the Convention Concerning the Compulsory Medical Examination of Children and Young People Employed at Sea 1921 (No. 16); the Convention Concerning Equality of Treatment for National and Foreign Workers as Regards Workmen's Compensation for Accidents 1925 (No. 19); the Convention Concerning Seamen's Articles of Agreement 1926 (No. 22); the Convention Concerning the Repatriation of Seamen 1926 (No. 23); the Convention Concerning the Creation of Minimum Wage Fixing Machinery 1928 (No. 26); the Convention Concerning the Making of the Weight of Heavy Packages Transported by Vessels 1929 (No. 27); the Convention Concerning the Protection against Accidents of Workers Employed in Loading or Unloading Ships 1929 (No. 32); the Convention Concerning the Employment of Women on Underground Work in Mines of all kinds 1935 (No. 45); the Convention Fixing the Minimum Age for Admission of Children to Industrial Employment 1937 (No. 59); the Convention Concerning Partial Revision of all Conventions Passed at the Former 28 Conferences and Others 1946 (No. 80).

In 1987 China ratified the Vocational Rehabilitation and Employment (Disabled Persons) Convention 1983 (No. 159) and in 1990 ratified the Convention Concerning Equal Remuneration for Men and Women Workers for Work of Equal Value 1951 (No. 100), and the Convention Concerning Tripartite Consultations to Promote the Implementation of International Labour Standards 1976 (No. 144).

74. China ratified the Convention concerning Employment Policy (No. 122) in 1997. In 1998, China ratified the Convention concerning Minimum Age for Admission of Employment 1976 (No. 138). In 2002, China ratified the Convention concerning the Prohibition and Elimination of the Worst Forms of Child Labour. In addition, the Chinese government has given priority to considering the ratification of conventions with respect to employment, occupational safety and health and social security.

§2. Domestic Sources

I. The Constitution

75. The Constitution is regarded as the 'Mother Law' in the Chinese legal system, due to its supremacy over other sources of normative rules, its substantive coverage of basic social, economic and political systems, and its special procedures for amendment. Instead of using the term 'sources of law', the Constitution refers to the legal system of the PRC as follows. Under the Constitution, law and statutes can be made by the National People's Congress and its Standing Committee; administrative regulations can be issued by the State Council or its ministries and commissions; local authorities, including legislative bodies and local governments at provincial level, can make local laws and regulations. The different levels of the normative rules in the hierarchy of legal system depend on the status of the authority which made the normative rules. Under the hierarchy of the system of normative rules stipulated by the Constitution, the local labour legislation enacted by the local legislative bodies and local governments at provincial level must not conflict with the laws and administrative regulations adopted by the national legislative body and central government, and the laws and administrative regulations must not conflict with the Constitution.

76. The fundamental economic, social and political system provided for in the Constitution as the 'Mother Law' establishes programmatic norms with which labour law and regulations are to comply as guiding principles. Specifically, in Chapter 2 of the Constitution, the basic rights and duties of citizens with regards to labour are proclaimed. They are, *inter alia*, the rights and duties of work, labour remuneration, labour discipline, working conditions, safety and labour protection, vocational training, the right to rest, the right to receive material assistance, freedom of association, equality between men and women, etc. These constitutionally entrenched provisions provide a very broad but profound basis for legislation, administrative regulations and local legislation in relation to labour issues. Furthermore, the Standing Committee of the National People's Congress is vested with the power to interpret the laws and the Constitution to maintain the consistency of the legislation. Because the Constitution only provides the abstract standard and its provisions lack justiciability, protection for the constitutional rights of citizens in connection with labour issues lies directly in concrete laws and regulations, provided that they are in compliance with the respective provisions of the Constitution which are subject to interpretation by the Standing Committee of the National People's Congress. However, it is rarely the case in practice that the Standing Committee of the National People's Congress exercises its power to declare a law or a relevant provision of a law unconstitutional and therefore void.

II. Laws

77. The National People's Congress (NPC) is authorized by the Constitution to enact and amend basic laws (statutes). Its Standing Committee may also enact and amend laws except those which may only be enacted by the National People's Congress itself. For example, the standing committee of the NPC promulgated the Civil Servant Act in 2005 which regulates the special labour relationship between a civil servant and a government agency. In addition, the standing committee of the NPC can also enact supplements and amendments to laws made by the NPC, if it is not in session and the supplements and amendments are not in conflict with the basic principles of the original laws made by the NPC. There is no difference in legal force between the basic statute and normal laws. The Labour Act was enacted by the Standing Committee of the NPC and has the same legal effect as the basic statutes. The Labour Act regulates all the basic aspects of labour law at the national level and is to be implemented in the single-item laws. Not only the general norms stipulated in provisions of the Labour Act need to be specified by the detailed implementing regulations, but also the national regulations need to be carried out by local law, taking into account local conditions and requirements.

III. Administrative Regulations Enacted by the State Council

78. In accordance with Article 89 of the Constitution, the State Council is vested with powers to adopt administrative measures, rules and regulations and issue decisions and orders in accordance with the Constitution and the laws.

79. The State Council may also adopt interim provisions on the matters that originally fall within the scope of enactment by the National People's Congress, which authorizes the State Council to regulate.

IV. Orders, Directives and Regulations of the Ministries and Commissions

80. In accordance with Article 90 of the Constitution, the ministries and commissions may issue orders, directives and regulations within their scope of administration and in accordance with the law and the administrative rules and regulations, decisions and orders issued by the State Council.

V. Other Sources

A. *Local Legislation*

81. Article 100 of the Constitution authorizes the local people's congress and its standing committee at provincial level to enact local legislation which must be not only in conformity with Constitution and national legislative enactment, but also in conformity with central government administrative regulations. Local legislation is required to be reported to the Standing Committee of the National People's Congress for the record. The Hong Kong and Macao Special Administrative Regions have their own legislative power to adopt legislation which will be subject to the Basic Law of Hong Kong of 1990 and Basic Law of Macao of 1993.

82. Local administrative regulations adopted by local governments are required to be reported to the State Council for the record. Where there is a conflict between the local administrative regulations and a ministry's regulations, the matter is handled and coordinated by the Legal Affairs Bureau of the State Council. If the Legal Affairs Bureau of the State Council fails to do so, the matter will be decided by the State Council.[17] In practice, local legislation has direct reference whenever the national laws are too broad and general, or when there are no relevant national laws at all. Where local law conflicts with national laws, the national laws must prevail according to Article 100 of the Constitution, except where local legislation is otherwise authorized.

B. Internal Rules

83. Internal rules must be understood in two senses. First, in China, some governmental regulations which are not available to the public may have a regulatory effect upon workers. The State Council and the Office of the State Council issue from time to time documents, known as internal documents, to the ministries or departments in charge and their local agencies with regard to specific policies which are subject to interpretation by the Office of the State Council. Such internal rules may also be issued by the government at ministerial level to local agencies at provincial level and further to county level to provide concrete criteria and methods in order to implement specific regulations.

84. Secondly, there are rules and regulations adopted by the employer and workers' congress which bind employees. Each employing unit has its own internal rules which directly affect the interests and rights as well as the obligations of workers.

C. Collective Agreements

85. Since the 1990s, the mechanism of collective consultation and collective agreement has been added to the contractual protection of labourers' rights after it had been recognized by the Trade Union Law and further developed by the Labour Act. As the collective agreement was practised only at the enterprise level, the employer had the option not to conclude a collective agreement and therefore the internal binding effect between the collective and individual contract remains limited. Terms set out in the collective agreement only serve as minimum standard for individual labour contracts in enterprises which have concluded such a collective agreement.

86. New amendments have been made to the Labour Contract Law which permits the binding power of a collective contract on the individual employment contract industry-wide or area-wide at the county level. However, the collective agreement is limited to such industries as construction, mining, catering services according to the Labour Contract Law.

17. See 1990 Provisions on Reporting Legislative Enactments and Administrative Regulations for the Record in *The Classified Assemblage of the Law of the PRC: Constitutional and Administrative Law* (Law Press 1994, Beijing), at p. 237.

§3. SECONDARY SOURCES

I. Legislative Interpretation

87. The demarcation between legislative, administrative and judicial interpretations is defined in accordance with the 1981 Resolution of the National People's Congress Standing Committee on Strengthening the Work of Interpretation of Laws.[18] In cases where the limits of provisions of laws and decrees need to be further defined, and/or additional stipulations need to be made, the Standing Committee of the National People's Congress will provide interpretations or make stipulations by means of decree (Art. 1). In cases where the limits of local legislation need to be further defined or additional stipulations need to be made, the standing committee of the people's congresses at provincial level which formulated this legislation will provide the interpretation or make the stipulation. Under Article 67 of the Constitution, the Standing Committee of the National People's Congress assumes the responsibility for interpretation of the Constitution and laws. In Chinese jurisprudence, the interpretation given by legislative bodies is referred to as legislative interpretation, which has superior force over judicial interpretation and administrative interpretation.

II. Judicial Interpretation

88. Only the Supreme People's Court may interpret points of law from the specific application of the law in judicial trials, while the Supreme People's Procuratorate may interpret points of law arising from the specific application of the law in procuratorial work. Both types of interpretation are referred to as judicial interpretations in Chinese jurisprudence. Where there is a difference in principle between the interpretations made by the Supreme People's Court and the Supreme People's Procuratorate, the Standing Committee of the National People's Congress shall be responsible for the interpretation and decision on the matter in question submitted to it.

89. Even though case law is not officially regarded as a source of Chinese law and is not legally binding, the Supreme People's Court's interpretations, including matters relating to labour law, either in the form of general interpretations of the application of the laws, or in the form of model cases in which standards and principles are established in a judgment on a particular leading case which are also deemed to be of nationwide importance, are published in the Gazette of the Supreme People's Court. This has a binding effect on the judicial practice of the local people's court at various levels which are not permitted to issue their own judicial interpretation documents according to the 1987 Reply of the Supreme People's Court

18. See *The Laws of the People's Republic of China 1979–1982*, Foreign Language Press Beijing 1987, at p. 251.

that local people's courts at various levels should not enact judicial interpretation documents.[19]

Recent noticeable judicial interpretations are the Interpretation of the Supreme People's Court on Several Issues in Application of Law for Hearing Labour Dispute Cases (2001), the Second Interpretation of the Supreme People's Court on Several Issues in Application of Law for Hearing Labour Dispute Cases (2006), the Third Interpretation of the Supreme People's Court on Several Issues in Application of Law for Hearing Labour Dispute Cases (2010) and the Fourth Interpretation of the Supreme People's Court on Several Issues in Application of Law for Hearing Labour Dispute Cases (2013). It is of practical relevance for lawyers and judges to follow the Supreme People's Court's reports on the leading labour law cases which indicate judicial application of the stipulations. On 8 November 2013, the Supreme People's Court announced the No. 18 guiding case with positive implications for judicial review of the labour rules and regulations in the trial of a specific labour dispute.

III. Administrative Interpretation

90. In accordance with the 1993 Notice of the Office of the State Council regarding the authority and procedures for the interpretation of administrative regulations,[20] the State Council is responsible for interpretation of those provisions of administrative regulations which need to be further defined or need supplementary stipulations. The government department in charge is responsible for interpretation of the application of the administrative regulation. Interpretation of the documents issued by the State Council and State Council's Office is the Office's responsibility.

---

19. See *Xin Zhongguo Sifa Jieshi Daquan* (*Complete Book of Judicial Interpretations in China Since 1949*), China Procuratorate Press 1990, at p. 1139.
20. See *The Classified Assemblage of the Law of the PRC: Constitutional and Administrative Law*, Law Press Beijing 1994, at p. 244.

Part I. The Individual Employment Relationship

Chapter 1. Definitions and Concepts

§1. Different Categories of Employees

I. Abolition of Status of Enterprises' Cadres and Workers

91. The Labour Act does not define the categories of employee with whom a labour contract is to be concluded. The long standing different categories between cadres who have a managerial, technical or bureaucratic position in enterprises and workers were abolished in accordance with the 1993 Notice on Issuance Shenzhen's Opinions on Abolition of the Status of Cadres and Workers in Enterprises in Order to Implement Contract Systems for All Employees,[21] issued by the Ministry of Labour. Under the Labour Act, it is intended that the labour contract system should apply to all employees regardless of their managerial, technical or administrative status in the enterprises; therefore, the Labour Act confirms the non-distinctive between normal workers and enterprises' cadres, in legal terms. It is clear that the intention of the Labour Act is to ensure that all employees who are subject to the Labour Act enjoy the protection of a labour contract. it is under intense discussion that the Labour Act should be applicable to workers in informal sectors, such as domestic workers, rural migrant workers and other types of workers who are not classified.

II. Factory Workers and Staff Employed in the Institutions

92. Categories can be drawn according to an employee's origins, employee's work unit, etc. According to an employee's work unit, the existing regulations define two basic categories of employees, i.e. factory workers and staff employed in state agencies, institutions and social organizations. Factory workers are generally referred to as industrial workers who are engaged in productive activities in state, collective or private enterprises. In state-owned enterprises (including state-run

21. See *Zhongguo Laudongfa Quanshu* [Complete Book of China's Labour Law] (Xinhua 1994), at p. 214.

farms), they are further defined as apprentices, permanent workers, temporary workers or peasant contract workers. Most professionals, ranging from bankers to sportsmen supported by the state, are treated as the staff of institutions.

III. Foreigners and Other Employees according to Employees' Origins

93. Foreign workers or expatriate employees and residents of Taiwan, Hong Kong and Macao employed in mainland China are subject to separate regulations on labour management. However, for the purposes of the contractual protection of employees, the Labour Act applies to employees in the territory of the People's Republic of China regardless of their nationality as long as a labour contract is established after the employment permit is granted by the Chinese authority. Nevertheless, there are uncertainties in practice because some rules specified in the Administrative Regulations on the Employment of Foreigners in China (2017 revision), issued by the Ministry of Human Resources and Social Security, impose restrictions on employment of foreigners. In general, foreign employees in China will also be governed by the Chinese Labour Act and Labour Contract Law and will enjoy the protection of a labour contract.

94. There are no categorized agricultural workers in China. Labourers engaged in farming work in rural areas are registered as peasants, who may be employed as peasant contracted workers in the state or private industry sector. Those peasants who work in enterprises run by the counties and towns will not be able to change their peasant resident status. In China the city residences and rural residences are strictly subject to registration of household. The Labour Contract Law does not cover peasants and farmers who are working for their contracted land. China's economy and society are dominated by dual economic and social systems today, i.e. two contrasting systems apply to rural regions and urban areas. In rural regions, the agricultural economy basically relies on contracted farm lands by households which are restrictively registered as rural residents. It is the plain fact that around 70 per cent of China's economy and society is within the regime of the agriculture system. The population in rural China is estimated to be approximately 600 million people according to the statistics of 2016 issued by the National Bureau of Statistics of China. However, the Labour Contract Law aims to protect the peasants and farmers working in the city by imposing a monetary penalty (amounting to two months' wages) on employers if they have not concluded a written contract upon employment of an employee for 1 month but fewer than 12 months.

§2. The Different Kinds of Individual Labour Contract

95. The definition of a labour contract is an agreement between the worker and the employing unit, establishing the employment relationship and specifying both parties' rights and obligations according to Article 16 of the Labour Act.

96. The Labour Act provides a comprehensive basis for the contract system to those individuals who fall within its scope. The Labour Act is not applicable to state public servants and peasants. Employees in state agencies, institutional organizations and social groups in which no labour contractual relationship has been established will not come under its jurisdiction.[22] Those enterprises, individual economic organizations inside the People's Republic of China (the employing unit) and employees who have labour relations with the employing unit will, however, fall within the ambit of the Labour Act. The classification of the individual contract and the contents of the contract required by the Labour Act are in principle applicable to all labour contracts of employees who are subject to this Labour Act. The Labour Contract Law intends to extend its application by providing that the conclusion, performance, amendment, rescission and termination of labour contracts by state authorities, institutions or social organizations on the one hand and workers with whom they establish labour relationships on the other hand, shall be handled pursuant to the Labour Contract Law.

I. The Individual Labour Contract for a Definite Period

97. In accordance with the Labour Act, a labour contract is classified as either a contract with a fixed term, an indefinite term or with terms depending on the time required to perform specific work (Article 20). Upon the termination of the fixed term contract, an extension may be made after an agreement has been reached between the two parties to the labour contract. This has become the most widely applicable type of contract in the labour market, because it can not only stabilize labour relations for a period of time but can also ensure and promote the mobility of labour forces. It is a significant development that the Labour Contract Law provides options for concluding fixed-term contracts, indefinite term contracts or contracts with a term subject to completion of a specific task. Importantly, if a fixed-term employment contract is concluded for two successive periods, an indefinite term contract must be granted if the employee so requests.

II. The Individual Labour Contract for an Indefinite Period

98. The Labour Act requires that if a worker has worked for the same employing unit for ten or more years, and when both parties to the labour contract agree to extend the contract, a labour contract of indefinite duration shall be made, if so requested by the worker. In foreign investment enterprises, the Chinese employee who, before being hired by the foreign investment enterprise, worked for ten years in the former Chinese enterprise which later became the party to the foreign investment enterprise, is entitled to an open-ended contract. The year of service of an employee who has worked for a previous employer which is merged or absorbed into another entity should be counted.

22. See Article 2 of the Labour Act in the *International Encyclopaedia for Labour Law and Industrial Relations* (Legislation) PR China, p. 101.

99. Since the implementation of the Labour Contract Law in 2008, two consecutive short-term contracts would result in a contract for an indefinite term. However, no minimum or maximum duration of these consecutive fixed-term contracts is required. Under the contract system, an employer and an employee, as parties to a labour contract, are still able to terminate or cancel the contract with indefinite term when the contractual or statutory terms and conditions for termination or cancellation are met.

III. Labour Contract with Terms Depending on the Time Required to Perform Specific Work

100. This refers to those contracts whose termination is subject to the completion of specific work, for example a construction project. This is by its nature a contract with fixed terms, but takes a different form.

IV. The Individual Labour Contract for Part-time Work and Secondment Arangement

101. There was a past practice that those temporary or seasonal workers who worked for state enterprises for up to one year were regarded as temporary workers in accordance with the Provisional Management Regulations on Temporary Workers in State Enterprises promulgated in 1989.[23] The temporary worker was in principle recruited from cities and towns. Where necessary, and upon approval by the labour administration of the municipalities, which are divided into districts, peasants can be recruited. However, upon expiry of the contract, the labour contract must be terminated. This practice was abolished in 2001 and replaced by a contract for part-time work. A part-time worker is referred to as an employee who works no more than 4 hours per day and 24 hours per week for a particular employer and who is remunerated by hourly rate. A part-time employee may have a labour contract with more than one employer. Either party to this part-time labour contract may terminate the contract without notice and economic compensation.

Atypical employment based on a secondment arrangement is regulated by a 2012 Amendment to the Labour Contract Law. The implementation of the 2012 amended Labour Contract Law is to reduce the scope of labour secondment and abuse of the secondment employment arrangement to employ rural migrant workers. A secondment labour contract or labour dispatch contract is a labour contract between an employee and a secondment company, which in turn dispatches the employee to work in place of a third party (seconded company). The use of labour secondment has become popular in China since 2008 as a countermeasure to the implementation of the Labour Contract Law. The 2012 amendment to the Labour Contract Law made a labour secondment arrangement strictly limited as to its use in three aspects. First, the secondment company is required to meet higher qualifications for being

23. See *Zhonggno Laodongfa Quanshu* [Complete Book of China's Labour Law] (Xinhua 1994), at p. 123.

able to dispatch the employees to work for a third party; secondly, an employment contract is to be established between the secondment company and seconded individuals who should be equally paid for equal work; thirdly, secondment arrangement should be made only for the works of temporary, auxiliary or alternative nature.

Secondment companies must enter into fixed-term labour contracts of two years or longer with seconded employees and pay remuneration on a monthly basis; during the period in which a seconded employee is not assigned any work duties, the secondment company should pay the employee remuneration on a monthly basis pursuant to the minimum wage standard stipulated by the local people's government.

In accordance with the Interim Provisions on Labour Dispatch (Art. 4), promulgated by the Ministry of Human Resources and Social Security in 2014, the number of seconded workers should not exceed 10 per cent of the total number of employees of an employer.

There was a specific labour contract for labourers from the countryside who were referred to as peasant contracted workers before 2008.[24] Those peasants who were contracted for more than one year enjoyed the same employment rights as normal urban contract workers. However, their peasant resident status remained unchanged. These contracted peasants were normally involved in manual work, construction projects and mining work. However, due to the recent development of the Labour Promotion Law and the Labour Contract Law, the previous unequal treatment of rural migrant workers lost its legal ground theoretically. The Labour Act and the Labour Contract Law should equally apply to the labourers from the countryside who are contracted as employees.

§3. The Trial Clause

102. Normally, a newly recruited employee will have a labour contract specifying a probationary period not exceeding six months, depending on the term of the contract, in accordance with Article 21 of the Labour Act. During the probationary period, both parties to the labour contract are allowed to terminate the contract. The employer may terminate the labour contract if the employee proves to be unqualified for the employment during the probationary period. During the probationary period neither employer nor employee is bound by the usual 30-day written notice period for the termination of the labour contract, but a 3-day notice is required in the event of termination by the employee. In addition, employers are not obliged to offer economic compensation for the termination of contract during the probationary period. The employee could request help from the trade union which has the right to raise objections if it considers the termination of a labour contract by the employer inappropriate under Article 30 of the Labour Act. In accordance with the Labour Contract Law (Art. 19), the probationary period may not exceed one month if a labour contract has a term of not less than three months but less than one year;

24. See the 1991 Regulations on Recruitment of Peasant Contract Workers in State Enterprises, *ibid.*, at p. 124.

if a labour contract has a term of more than one year and less than three years, the probationary period may not exceed two months; and if a labour contract has a term of not less than three years or is open-ended, the probationary period may not exceed six months. Just one probationary period can be stipulated in a labour contract. The wage amount of a worker during his/her probationary period shall not be less than the lowest wage amount for the same job position in the employer's organization or 80 per cent of the wage amount agreed in the labour contract and shall not be less than the minimum wage standard of the locality of the employer.

§4. Requirements for the Conclusion of a Valid Individual Labour Contract

I. The Legal Capacity to Conclude an Individual Labour Contract

103. Under Chinese labour law, citizens aged 16 are deemed to have the 'capacity of right to work' and the 'capacity of the act to work' with which the individual can assume his or her rights of work and perform the duty of work under the individual labour contract. Article 15 of the Labour Act provides that an employing unit shall be prohibited from recruiting minors who are under 16 years of age. Under Chinese civil law, citizens who have reached the age of 18 have full legal capacity, which is two years later than the 'capacity of the act to work'.

104. In concluding the labour contract, the relevant employment policy and law will apply to handicapped persons, ethnic minorities or soldiers retired from active service. In principle the subject of the individual labour contract is protected from discrimination because of nationality, race, sex or religious belief.

105. A qualified employing unit which can conclude a labour contract is normally required by Chinese law to be a legal person or a private enterprise employer who has citizenship.

A. *Minors*

106. State approval and examination will be required for the employment of minors who are under 16 years of age who are committed to artistic, athletic and special handicraft work. In accordance with Regulations on Banning the Use of Child Labour 1991 (revised as of 2002 on the same matter),[25] child labourers and children under the age of 16 having a working relationship with units or individuals and engaged in economic income-earning labour or doing self-employed labour are referred to as juveniles. However, child labour excludes those who are under the age of 16 participating in family work, school organized work study or supplementary labour permitted by provincial governments if it is not harmful to their physical and

25. See *International Encyclopaedia for Labour Law and Industrial Relations* (Legislation) PR China, p. 47.

mental health and within their capacities. These regulations further impose duties on parents and guardians not to allow children under the age of 16 to work as child labourers.

107. According to Article 94 of the Labour Act, a fine can be imposed on the employer who illegally recruits minors, and the business licence of the employer may be revoked where the circumstances are serious.

B. Women

108. Women who are party to a labour contract are entitled to special protection under the Rules on the Labour Protection of Female Workers 1988 which was replaced by the same rules in 2012. The purpose of the rules is not to limit female citizens committing themselves in special work. It is forbidden to employ female workers to work in mines or inside wells, to perform manual labour that requires grade four stamina as stipulated by the state. During female menstruation, females do not have to work at higher altitude, under low temperature or in cold water or perform manual labour that requires grade three stamina as stipulated by the state. There are further provisions to protect pregnant women from committing themselves to manual labour which is totally unsuitable for them. It further regulates the female employees' legitimate rights for a secured employment and related leave entitlements and employers' corresponding obligations.

109. In accordance with Article 95 of the Labour Act, a fine can be imposed for violation of the provision regarding protection of women and minors, and compensation is to be paid to the women and minors for the damage caused.

II. Consent

110. A valid labour contract is required to be concluded based on the consent of the parties to the contract. As a labour contract is an agreement between two parties, its conclusion and amendment must be made on the basis of the principles of equal, voluntary and mutual consent; in addition, its content and the procedure for the conclusion of the contract must not contravene the provisions of the law and administrative regulations (Art. 17 of the Labour Act). Article 18 of the Labour Act further defines the invalid contract in two respects:

(a) the content of the labour contract violates the law or administrative regulations;
(b) the procedure of concluding the labour contract is against the principles of voluntary and mutual consent by reason of force or intimidation. Therefore, both the procedure to reach the consent and the content of the consent reached by the party must be in conformity with the law and administrative regulations.

III. Written Form with Mandatory Provisions

111. In China, the labour contract must be in written form. In general, without a written contract, no social security coverage and calculation of the years of service will apply to workers. Therefore, the labour legislation requires that the written labour contract be concluded for the establishment of an employment relationship. In accordance with the Labour Contract Law, if the employer fails to enter into the written contract with a worker for 12 months or more, a contract of an indefinite term shall be deemed to have been concluded. On 18 January 2013, the Supreme People's Court promulgated the Interpretation of Several Issues concerning the Application of Law in Labour Dispute Cases, according to which any verbal changes of labour contract without written form should be deemed to be valid if the change has been in effect for more than one month, as long as the changed contents comply with laws, administrative regulations, state policies and public order and good morals. The written contract follows the model contract provided and recommended by the local labour administrations. This is also the practice for some other kinds of Chinese domestic contracts. The model form is designed to contain all mandatory provisions and to standardize the format of contracts for ease of administration. Due to the complexity of the labour market, the use of the the model contract designated by the responsible authority is becoming less popular.

112. In accordance with Article 19 of the Labour Act, the mandatory provisions include the following:

(a) duration of the labour contract;
(b) job description;
(c) labour protection and conditions;
(d) labour remuneration;
(e) labour discipline;
(f) conditions for the termination of the labour contract; and
(g) responsibilities in the event of a contravention of the labour contract.

It is worth noticing that the Labour Contract Law restricts the use of *laissez-faire* doctrine in respect of 'conditions for termination of the labour contract' or disciplinary measurements. Company rules and regulations could be served as part of agreement binding on both parties to the labour contract only when such company rules and regulations are formulated with statutory required procedures.

The Labour Contract Law further stresses that a labour contract shall specify the detailed information about employer and employee, the provisions on social insurance matter for the employee and protection measures against occupational hazards, etc.

113. There is some room left for negotiation on other clauses based on the second paragraph of Article 19 of the Labour Act, which provides that parties may consult and agree on other items of a labour contract in addition to the compulsory clauses specified above. In practice, the parties usually have to reach agreement on the employee's rights and obligations with respect to probation, training, confidentiality, non-competition, etc. and to changing of or transfer between employing units; it is quite often the case in disputes that an employee is sent out by the employer to receive training given by other employers in another province, but after training, stays with the training unit or joins another employing unit while ignoring the original labour contract. The Labour Contract Law allows an employment contract to stipulate certain required years of service of an employee for the employer who pays for the training of the employee. In addition, the settlement of labour disputes is usually provided for in the labour contract. The Labour Act and the Labour Contract Law particularly allow the conclusion of a confidentiality clause and/or a non-competition clause to protect the commercial secrets of the employer.

IV. Certification or Confirmation Requirement

114. A labour contract used to require certification by the local regulations; the labour administration, as the administrative supervision organ for labour contracts, could request or instruct the parties to the contract to make necessary changes or to conclude a new contract if the initial contract was found to be in contravention of the law.[26] The certification is no longer required by the Labour Contract Law.

V. Validity and Binding Force

115. An invalid labour contract shall not be legally binding from the time it is concluded. If part of a labour contract is found to be invalid, the remainder is still valid, provided that the validity of the remainder is not affected by the invalid part. As a matter of law, only if arbitration or court proceedings are initiated, will the validity of a labour contract be decided or confirmed. However, it remains unclear what form restitution/compensation would take for the damaged party of the invalid contract when an invalid labour contract is void *ab initio*.[27] At least the Labour Contract Law makes it clear that if a labour contract is confirmed as invalid and the employee has already performed labour, the employer must pay remuneration to the employee. The amount of remuneration shall be determined with reference to the remuneration of employees in the same or a similar position with the employer.

26. See Implementing Measures for the Certification of the Labour Contract, 1992, in *Complete Book of China's Labour Law* (Xinhua, 1994) at p. 216.
27. See Article 18 of the Labour Act in the *International Encyclopaedia for Labour Law and Industrial Relations* [Legislation] PR China, p. 101.

Chapter 2. Duties of the Parties during Employment

§1. Statutory Duties and Contractual Obligations of the Parties

116. Statutory duties imposed on the parties and the contractual obligations of the parties in the course of the employment relationship are interrelated. The former creates the statutory limitation binding on employers and employees at large, while the latter creates binding obligations upon particular parties to individual contracts which must not be over the statutory limitation. The statutory rights and duties of employees and employers during employment apply to employment relations regardless of the industry and the trade in which the employment relations have arisen and regardless of the ownership of the enterprises or sectors, for example, public, state owned, private or foreign invested. Furthermore, statutory duties regarding working time, occupational safety and health, remuneration, social insurance etc., further provided for in the different chapters of the Labour Act have direct reference to the parties in concluding and performing the labour contract.

117. The contractual rights and duties of the parties form the substantial content of the labour contract. The status of employees in employer-dominated labour relations results in an employee-protective orientated contractual relationship, which is essentially different from a merely commercial contractual relationship. Obligations of the employee to the labour contract would not accordingly raise the employer's corresponding right without statutory limitation. The employee's right is protected not only by the performance of the corresponding duty of the employer, to the extent imposed by the contract, but also by the performance of the employer's statutory duties.

118. It is often the case that the individual labour contract does not refer directly to the employee's collective rights for example, the right to join a trade union, trade union rights, democratic management, equal consultation rights, etc. It certainly does not mean that the employer has no duty to ensure that such rights are enjoyed by workers. Article 4 of the Labour Act imposes on employers the statutory duty to establish and improve a system of rules and regulations in accordance with the law, and to safeguard workers' enjoyment of labour rights and performance of labour duties.

119. With respect to the rights of the employee in employment relations, by and large, employees are granted by law the freedom of job selection and resignation, no employment discrimination and no forced labour. Article 3 of the Labour Act guarantees equality of employment opportunity, the right to choose one's occupation, to receive labour remuneration, to rest and have holidays, to enjoy safety at work and health protection, to undertake vocational training, to ensure social insurance and welfare, and the right to request the settlement of labour disputes and other labour rights stipulated by law.

120. With respect to the statutory duties of the employee, the second paragraph of Article 3 of the Labour Act further stipulates that a worker must complete his working tasks, improve his vocational skills, implement safety at work and health regulations, and observe labour discipline and professional code of conduct.

§2. Duties of the Employee

I. Duty to Work

121. As stated above, work is not only regarded as a right but also as a duty of Chinese citizens. 'Duty to work' here refers to the duty to perform work in the context of individual labour contracts which stipulate specific tasks, occupations and work qualities entrusted to employees. It involves the honest performance of the worker's obligations in good faith, while observing the regulated technical and occupational standards for the accomplishment of specific tasks. Apart from the qualitative aspect of the tasks, the employee must undertake a specific quantity or volume of work or number of tasks under the individual labour contract, i.e. the output that the worker should achieve.

122. The duty to observe labour discipline and professional conduct is essential to ensure the process of production in a regulated manner. For example, employees are obliged to observe working hours, to follow the instructions of the supervisor and to comply with the enterprise's internal rules and regulations. As mentioned above, before the promulgation of the Labour Contract Law (2008), the provision of any employer's internal labour rules and regulations in practice might be part of the labour contract and provided as an attachment thereto. Thus, the obligation for the employee was to abide by labour rules and regulations as part of the performance of the labour contract itself. In order to maintain the normal orders of production, the 1986 Regulations on the Dismissal of Workers and Staff for Violation of Labour Discipline in State Enterprises[28] which was promulgated by the State Council, had stipulated that employees who had, among other things, refused to accept a normal work transfer, or were involved in corruption, theft, gambling or misuse of their position which did not rise to the level of criminal misconduct, disturbances or fighting which caused a serious breach of the peace, extreme disrespect towards the enterprises' clients, frequent arguments or quarrels with customers, violation of operating rules which damaged equipment or tools or which wasted materials or energy thereby causing economic losses and other similar instances of serious misconduct would be subject to administrative penalties and further to dismissal if education and other administrative penalties failed. These regulations served as guidance until they were replaced in 2001 and abolished in 2008. With the introduction of Labour Contract Law, enterprise labour disciplinary rules must be approved through transparent and democratic procedures by the

28. See International Labour Office, Legislative Series 1986, China, p. 3.

employee assembly or employee congress before becoming binding on the employees. Importantly, for large sized organizations with subsidiaries all over the world, the group directives are not automatically binding on local operations in each jurisdiction, unless they are adapted to become local company regulations through transparent procedures as required.

123. Occupational standards must be maintained and proper conduct must be of the standard to meet professional requirements. These are actually interrelated obligations of the employees. Professionals are called upon by the law and regulations to observe professional ethics. The occupational standards for doctors, lawyers, teachers, professors, accountants, bankers etc., will be subject to their own regulated professional conduct as well as relevant statutes for each profession.

124. The duty to carry out safety procedures at work is explicitly provided for in Article 56 of the Labour Act. Workers are strictly duty bound to abide by the rules for safety operations in the course of work.

II. Duty to Observe Commercial Secrets

125. Article 22 of the Labour Act particularly stipulates that labour contracts may include a clause on the confidentiality of commercial secrets imposing an obligation on the employee to keep the commercial secrets of the employer. For different professions, specific professional secrets are also protected from exposure, as well as misuse during employment and after termination of the labour contract. It is especially significant, from the legal point of view, to stipulate the confidentiality obligation of employees being kept in force for such periods of time after the contract itself expires or terminates so as to provide sufficient measures to prevent former employees from exposing or using commercial secrets for commercial purpose or other purposes which might infringe upon the rights and interests of the former employer. However, practice shows that the confidentiality clause is of little effect. Apart from a sophistication of the general legal protection against exposing the former employer's commercial secrets, it remains largely a case of the employee's moral obligation in this matter. Nevertheless, the Labour Act imposes on the employee not only the duty to respect and keep commercial secrets, but also intends that the parties to the labour contract determine the detailed content, methods and time limit of commercial secrets.

III. Liability

126. Administrative and economic liability will be assumed by the employee for non-performance of the obligation of the individual labour contract, especially non-observance of labour discipline, exposure of commercial secrets and non-compliance with the statutory condition of termination of the contract.

127. Regulations on Punishment and Awards to the Enterprise's Employee of 1982[29] were abolished in 2008, with the following administrative measures stated in these Regulations being widely adopted in practice:

- warnings;
- recording employee's misconduct;
- demoting to a lower rank;
- dismissal from one's particular post;
- continuing employment relations subject to further examination; and
- dismissal from the enterprise.

Due to the implementation of the Labour Act and the Labour Contract Law, administrative measures are largely subject to the stipulations of the labour contract whereby specific measures set out in the rules and regulations of the employer must be observed as a part of the contractual stipulations in dealing with a specific disciplinary violation.

128. The above-mentioned progressive disciplinary procedures are quite typical when making enterprise regulations. Before administrative measures are taken, informal warnings and educational measures should be taken to help change the behaviour of employees who violate labour discipline, disobey their supervisor, disturb the production order by getting involved in fighting and other disturbances, misuse their position, violate technical, operational and safety rules, waste raw materials, damage equipment and commit other serious misconduct, etc. In practice, the list of misconduct may get longer, so it is advisable to formulate such incidents of violation or misconduct clearly and specifically in the company rules and regulations.

129. In accordance with the Employment Dispute Mediation and Arbitration Law, the employer shall bear the burden of prove proving that the disciplinary procedures imposed on the employee is justified, based on existing rules and regulations and with solid evidence. Article 22 of the Labour Act and Article 23 of the Labour Contract Law state that the employer and the employee may, in a labour contract, stipulate the matters relating to employer's trade secrets and the intellectual property. Any charge against an employee for his or her violation of the employer's trade secrets and the intellectual property rights as detailed in the labour contract would be better determined and established by the arbitration or the court if such detailed stipulations also provided the penalty and compensation for the breach of contract.

130. Employees are liable for economic compensation for wasting materials and damage to equipment or property caused by violation of the technical and safety regulations. The above measures in practice have been less and less frequently adopted, because both the Labour Act and the Labour Contract Law allow the termination of an employment contract with an employee who has seriously violated

29. See *Complete Book of China's Labour Law* (Xinuhua 1994), at p. 941.

the rules and regulations of the employer (including the violation of discipline set out in the rules and regulations of the employer).

131. Article 103 of the Labour Act provides that where a worker breaches the confidentiality clause of his labour contract thereby causing the employing unit to suffer economic loss, he shall be liable for compensation in accordance with the law. Article 118 of the General Principle of the Civil Law of the PRC 1986[30] protects the individual's and the legal person's right to authorship (copyright), patent right, right to the exclusive use of a trademark, right of discovery, right of invention or other rights pertaining to scientific or technical achievements from infringement in the way of plagiarism, falsification or imitation. The infringed party has the right to request that the infringement be stopped, the effects of the infringement eliminated and the damage compensated for. Article 9 of the Law against Unfair Competition 1993[31](amendment in 2017) defined the term commercial secrets as technical and management information which is unknown to the public and can produce economic benefits and have therefore been kept secret. In line with the Labour Contract Law, imposing an obligation of confidentiality and non-competition on an employee will result in monthly economic compensation payable by the employer to the employee for a duration not exceeding two years as the maximum period of the non-competition upon the end of employment.

132. Economic compensation can be increased if the employee terminates the labour contract in violation of the condition for termination stipulated by the Labour Act thereby causing the employing unit economic losses. In many cases, the employee leaves the employer for another job and leaves no word of his whereabouts. In practice, it remains problematic that the employer's economic loss caused in such a case should be compensated for by the employee since this can hardly be implemented. On the other hand, with the implementation of the social insurance system, the employee on leave must inform his or her employer, for he or she may transfer his or her social insurance only with the release certificate of his or her existing employer. The labour authority has held that the employer should not take any punitive measures against the families or the relatives of an employee who has left his/her job.[32]

§3. Duty of the Employer

I. Duty of Job Security

133. In China, state enterprises are still responsible, to some extent, for taking job assignment quotas according to the state plan; in other words, the employer, especially in the public sector and in state-owned enterprises has the duty to employ those who are assigned a job by the state. In addition, state enterprises are still

30. See *The Laws of the Peoples' Republic of China 1983–1986* (Beijing 1987), at p. 225.
31. See *China Laws for Foreign Business, Business Regulation* (CCH International), pp. 16–640.
32. See *Complete Book of China's Labour Law* (Xinhua 1994), at p. 1229.

responsible for securing jobs for existing employees, even though state enterprises have been authorized to have more autonomy in recruitment and dismissal of the employees.

134. After the employment contract system has been extended to all employees, the employer as a party is in a position to terminate the employment relationship in accordance with the law or by agreement between the two parties. However, the statutory condition for termination of employment relation by the employer must be met. In the case of the reduction of personnel, the 1994 Regulations concerning the Reduction of Personnel for Economic Reasons in Enterprises[33] were adopted by the Ministry of Labour to implement the Labour Act provisions regarding employers' rights to reduce the number of their personnel due to the employer being in serious economic difficulties or during the period of statutory restructuring on the verge of bankruptcy (Art. 27 of Labour Act). However, the employing unit is further required to give priority to those reduced personnel to be re-employed if the same employer recruits personnel within six months after such laying-off has taken place.

135. The 1993 Regulations concerning Arrangement of Redundancy in the State-Owned Enterprises[34] were adopted to cope with the transition of enterprises' management mechanism. State enterprises were permitted to be reorganized, during which time issues of redundancy were handled in a dogmatic way in accordance with these regulations. Enterprises adopted numerous measures, such as extending maternity leave by increasing it from a regulated 90 days to up to two years, granting paid holiday but only paying about 50–70 per cent of the basic wage for living expenses, and allowing workers who were five years from retirement to leave their positions to 'recuperate' at home in accordance with the 1993 Regulations concerning Arrangement of Redundancy in State-Owned Enterprises. Government dogmatic policy requires 'internal digestion as a rule, dismissal (or laying-off) as an exception' which means that the employer must settle surplus labour within the enterprises or reallocate jobs as much as possible so as to ensure low redundancy and less social unrest. Such an approach brought experience not only to state-owned enterprises, but also to enterprises with different ownerships.

II. Duty to Ensure Labour Safety and to Provide Working Conditions and Training

136. In order to ensure that the employee performs his or her labour duties, the employer is obliged to provide specific work in accordance with the labour contract and to give the workers the necessary instruction and training, and to explain the relevant technical and safety rules and regulations. Labour safety and working conditions must be provided by the employer in conformity with state regulations. This includes the employer's duty to take necessary measures to prevent accidents in the

33. See China Update: the PRC, *Labour Law* (Asia Law and Practice 1995), at p. 118.
34. See *Complete Book of China's Labour Law* (Xinhua 1994), at p. 148.

course of work and reduce occupational hazards.[35] Physical examinations must be conducted on a regular basis for workers engaged in operations considered hazardous. The 2002 Production Safety Law imposes more specific obligations on business operators to ensure safe production and grants rights to employees in securing their safety at the work, including their right to stop working or right to leave the working place in case of emergency. In addition, Article 20 of the 1996 Vocational Educational Law imposes the obligation on enterprises to provide vocational education and training for their employees.

III. Duty to Pay Remuneration

137. The employer has the duty to pay remuneration to the employees for the employees' contribution to work. Wage and salary distribution must conform to the principal of distribution on the basis of the amount of work, equal pay for equal work (Art. 46 of the Labour Act). The duty for the employer to pay employees as referred to in the labour contract must conform to statutory provisions. First, wages and salaries must be paid only in legal tender, instead of wages in kind or securities, on a monthly basis. Therefore, the employer should not delay or deduct the payment including payment for overtime to the employees. Payment or part of the payment made in the form of a commodity to employees is regarded as nonperformance of the duty of the employer. Secondly, wages must be also paid by the employer for statutory rest days, holidays, marriage and bereavement leave as well as during periods when workers take part in social activities in accordance with the law (Art. 51 of the Labour Act). In accordance with the Labour Contract Law, a court may issue a payment order to an employer who delays a wage payment or does not pay wages in full.

IV. Duty Regarding Social Security Contributions for the Employee

138. Chapter 9 of the Labour Act provides a legal framework for the establishment of a social security system which covers risks such as unemployment, old age, sickness, work-related injuries and childbirth. Except for the types of insurance stated in Articles 70 and 73, the Labour Act lays down the principles of contributions to the social insurance funds, consolidated financing, administration (Arts. 71 and 72) and supervision of the funds (Art. 74). In accordance with 1999 Regulations on Unemployment Insurance (replacing the 1993 Regulations on Unemployment Insurance for Employees of State-owned Enterprises),[36] which extend unemployment insurance to all the eligible insured), an employer in urban areas must pay 2 per cent of its total payroll as the unemployment insurance premiums, while the employee must pay 1 per cent of his/her respective wages. Meanwhile,

35. Industrial fatalities grew alongside the economic boom; *see* reports in *China Daily* (Beijing) 23 June and 12 September 1992; *Financial Times* (London) 24/25 April 1993.

36. See *International Encyclopaedia of Labour Law and Industrial Relations* [Legislation] PR China, p. 74.

the Standing Committee of the NPC adopted the Social Insurance Law in 2010, effective 2011, which regulates and standardizes national-wide social security scheme covering unemployment, the basic medical care, work-related injury, old-age and childbirth. With historical importance, pursuant to the Resolution of the State Council on Restructuring of Old-Age Insurance for Workers and Staff in Enterprises of 1991,[37] a three-tier pension scheme has been introduced. The unified statutory old-age insurance funds have been established and managed at the provincial level since 1991. To the statutory old-age insurance funds, contribution rates paid by the employers differ from region to region. The three-tier pension scheme under the Resolution is applied to employees in state enterprises and may be applicable to employees in collective-owned undertakings, but is not applicable to workers in rural enterprises and peasants.[38] It has become the practice that employers are duty bound to contribute to work-related injury insurance and childbirth insurance, while the state, employer and individual employee share the premiums for unemployment, old-age and medical insurance. Housing reform, by way of establishment of housing provident fund for the benefit of eligible employees, has greatly relieved the state enterprise's burden of providing housing for employees. The Regulations on Housing Provident Fund (promulgated in 1999 and amended in 2012) as administrative provisions apply to all employees and employers.

139. Although the 1953 Labour Insurance Regulations as a whole are still in effect, some provisions have in fact been replaced by recent practices, such as those regarding the financing of statutory insurance funds, provisions for medical care benefits and provisions concerning retirement and invalidity benefits. The Social Insurance Law sums up over six decades' reform experiences in transforming the paternalistic labour insurance system into a universal social security system.

V. Liability

140. In accordance with the Labour Act, the legal liability of the employer includes administrative liability, economic liability and criminal liability.

141. Administrative penalties will be imposed upon employers who formulate labour rules and regulations in violation of state law or regulations. Such administrative penalties include warning and rectification of the situation by the labour administrative department (Art. 89 of the Labour Act). The same administrative penalties can be imposed by the labour administrative department for the violation of the regulated working time by the employer (Art. 90 of the Labour Act). Administrative penalties will be imposed if employers violate provisions regarding employers' duties with respect to labour safety and social security. Some other detailed rules of administrative penalties for the violation of the Labour Act will be discussed below.

37. See *Complete Book of China's Labour Law* (Xinhua 1994) at p. 103.
38. See Chen, Ke, 'Pension Reform in the PRC: A Legal Analysis' in 4 *Deutsche Rentenversicherung* 1995, at pp. 284–299.

142. Criminal liability may be imposed upon employers who force workers to work by means of violence, threats or illegal restrictions of personal freedom, insult, physically punish, beat, illegally search or detain employees (Art. 102 of the Labour Act). The public security authority may detain the responsible persons for up to 15 days or impose a fine or issue a warning to persons who commit the above-mentioned violations (or infringements). In particular, the Amendments to the Criminal Law (VIII) in 2011 stipulate that deliberately not paying wages to employees will be considered a crime.

143. Economic liability will arise from the conclusion of invalid labour contracts and termination of labour contracts. Article 97 of the Labour Act provides that compensation shall be payable to the employee for losses caused by an invalid contract for reasons attributable to the employing unit. Where the employee has the right to conclude a labour contract with the employer who deliberately delays concluding the labour contract, the labour administrative department may order the employer to make a rectification and, if damage has been caused to the workers, the employing unit will be liable for compensation. Joint and several liabilities for compensation in accordance with the law may be imposed upon the employer who recruits a worker whose existing labour contract has not been terminated, thereby causing the former employing unit to suffer economic loss (Art. 99 of the Labour Act). Provisions regarding severance payment will be discussed in further detail. In addition, the employer will be liable for economic compensation and damages if he fails to perform his duty to pay remuneration to an employee.

Chapter 3. Working Time and Leave, Sunday Rest, Annual Vacation, Holidays, Educational Leave

§1. Working Time

I. Definitions

144. Working time means the regulated time spent by a labourer on working, including daily working hours and the weekly working days. Regulated working time covers the following issues: the length of working hours, the calculation of working time, overtime, intervals during the work or break, rest, statutory holiday and so on. The determination of working time is regarded not only as a precondition for performance of work but also as a precondition for safeguarding the employee's right to rest. The principles of determination of working time and rest time are as follows. First, they must safeguard the right to rest and protect labourers' health; secondly, they must ensure completion of work or production tasks; thirdly, the regulated working time is an up limit of the standard working time. Employers may adopt non-standard working time within the legal framework or shortened working time to cope with the need of the operation.

145. The Labour Act confirms the new working hours system established under the State Council's Regulations governing Working Hours for Workers of 1994,[39] i.e. at the most 8 hours daily, with a weekly average of 44 hours for employees in all enterprises, state organs and other working units, including foreign invested enterprises and foreign companies in China. The State Council Regulations, amended in 1995, stipulate that the working time shall be 8 hours per day and 40 hours a week. For part-time work, according to the Labour Contract Law, a worker is generally averages not more than 4 hours of work per day and not more than an aggregate 24 hours of work per week for the same employer. (For a detailed description, please refer to paragraph 102.) Furthermore, the Labour Act provides that employees are entitled to paid annual vacation. For the first time since the founding of the People's Republic of China, Chinese employees have enjoyed a two-day weekend every other week and a paid annual vacation for up to 15 days depending upon seniority. See also paragraphs 152 and 158.

Subject to the Labour Act, enterprises not able to implement standard working hour system due to a feature of their operation may adopt other working and rest systems. In accordance with the 1994 Approving Procedures for Implementation of Flexible Working Hour and Integrated Working Hour Policies, the non-standard working hour system includes flexible working hours, integrated working hours and a piece wage system. The implementation of both flexible working hours and integrated working hours requires approval by the labour administration. The flexible working hour system is a special working time arrangement applicable to limited circumstance. The integrated working hour system is referred to as working hours

39. These regulations were amended and promulgated again on 25 March 1995. See *International Encyclopaedia of Labour Law and Industrial Relations* (Legislation)] PR China, p. 119.

calculated in a given time span, namely, one month or one quarter or even two quarters. The integrated working hour is applied to industries with seasonal peak and enterprises with unbalanced customer orders. As for the piece wage system, labour remuneration is based on the volume that the employee achieves with a limitation on the unit rate.

II. Content of Limitations

A. Daily

146. In general, a daily working time of eight hours is the norm in government agencies, social organizations, enterprises, institutions and other organizations.

147. In the event of an emergency or special circumstances, daily working hours can be extended in consultation with employees and trade unions; however, the daily extension of working hours must not generally exceed one hour per day. Where it is necessary to extend working hours for special reasons, daily working hours may be extended by no more than three hours daily, up to 36 hours per month, provided that the health of the employee is ensured (Art. 41 of the Labour Act).

148. The maximum daily and weekly working hours shall be applied as a principle to those employees who are engaged in piece work. The determination of their working hours may be flexible but must not exceed a total weekly working hour limit.

B. Weekly

149. Weekly working hours have generally been reduced from an upper limit of 44 hours weekly, as stipulated in the Labour Act, to 40 hours according to the Regulations of the State Council governing Working Hours for Workers, effective from 1 May 1995 as an amendment to the 1994 Regulations. These regulations stipulate that the latest date for its implementation by institutions was 1 July 1996 and the latest date for implementation by enterprises was 1 May 1997. It is stipulated that government organs and institutions must take unified working hours with Saturday and Sunday being the weekly rest days. Institutions and enterprises which are unable to implement the 40-hour weekly working times may arrange alternative rest days.

150. From the historic point of view, China has made great progress in reducing weekly working hours from its previous 48 hours which had been in practice since the early 1950s to 44 hours in March 1994 and a further reduction to 40 hours in May 1995. It indicates that the government has gradually adopted international labour standards while taking account of China's actual situation.

151. The weekly working time can only be extended up to a total of 36 hours per month as stipulated by the Labour Act. However, in accordance with Article 42 of the Labour Act the limitation for the extension of working time will not apply under the following circumstances: first, in the event of natural disasters, accidents or other reasons which threaten the lives, health and property of the workers and where urgent action is necessary or must be taken; secondly, where urgent repairs are required due to malfunctioning of production equipment, communication or transport lines or public facilities affecting production and public interests; or thirdly, other circumstances provided by the law or administrative regulations.

§2. Weekly Rest and Holiday

I. Weekly Rest

152. Since 1995, two days of weekly rest had been practiced in those enterprises and employing units which implemented five days of weekly working time. Those enterprises and employing units which were unable to practise five working days per week would adopt two days of weekly rest every other week. Except for the government and institutions which are obliged to take Saturday and Sunday as weekly rest days, alternative days taken as weekly rest days may be decided by other working units. It was after 1 May 1997 all employing units adopted two days of weekly rest for employees. The two-day weekends have become common practice in China for around 20 years.

II. Public Holidays

153. Seven days of public holiday apply to all employees nationwide. Article 40 of the Labour Act provides that national festival days (the New Year, the Chinese Spring Festival days, International Labour Day and National Day) and other days stipulated by law are public holidays which shall be arranged for employees. When such holidays happen to be on a weekly rest day, an extra weekday's holiday should be given. More specific provisions can be found in the Measurements for Holiday Leave in National Public Holidays, Festival Days and Commemoration Days (revised in December 2007).

154. In addition to a one-day holiday on 1 January of the Gregorian calendar year, employees in China enjoy another three days holiday for the Chinese new year – the spring festival which is on the first, the second and the third day of the first month of the lunar calendar new year. 1 May is a one-day holiday for International Labour Day. 1, 2 and 3 October are holidays for National Day. One day's holiday is given for mid-autumn day, dragon boating day and tomb sweeping day respectively according to the Chinese lunar calendar.

155. Some other statutory holidays apply only to certain employees, such as Women's Day on 8 March for female workers; Youth Day on 4 May for young workers; Commemoration Day for the Founding of the People's Liberation Army on 1 August for the army and other military agencies. In addition, there are holidays granted only to ethnic minorities according to particular customs.

III. Paid Leave

A. Annual Vacation

156. Annual vacation with pay for employees has been widely implemented since the Labour Act came into effect. The period of vacation varies from region to region. Those employees who have worked continuously for more than one year will be entitled to a paid annual vacation, the length thereof depending upon the length of service with the employing units. In 2007, the State Council promulgated Regulations on Paid Annual Leave for Employees, according to which if an employee has worked continuously one full year but less than 10 years, the annual paid leave is 5 days; if an employee has worked 10 full years but less than 20 years, the annual paid leave is 10 days; if an employee has worked for 20 full years, the annual paid leave is 15 days. The annual paid vacation was further clarified in the Implementation Measures on Paid Annual Leave for Employees of Enterprises, issued by Ministry of Human Resources and Social Security (18 September 2008).

B. Home Visits

157. The practice of home visits was popular in China in the planned economy system, in which employees worked in place subject to state job assignment. The current practice originates from 1958 regulations which have been replaced by the 1981 Resolution of the Standing Committee of the National People's Congress Approving the Provisions of the State Council for Home Leave for Workers and Staff.[40] Statutory paid home leave is not only for a visit to the spouse but also to the parents. Employees of government agencies, organizations, state enterprises and institutions who have worked for more than one year are entitled to visit their spouses or parents who live too far to visit during the weekend or on a public holiday. A spouse visit is granted for one of the spouses for a 30-day paid leave annually. Married employees are granted a 20-day visit to parents once every four years. For unmarried employees a 20-day paid leave must be granted each year for a visit to their parents.

158. The calculation of days for home visits includes public holidays, but does not count days spent for travelling. Home visits were designed to compensate for the situation in which families have been torn apart due to working and living far apart, resulting from the previous system of job assignment and mobilization of labourers to work in the remote areas, for political, military or other reasons. Since

40. See *The Laws of the People's Republic of China 1979–1982* (Foreign Language Press Beijing 1987), at p. 241.

the 1980s the government has adopted policies to reunite spouses who work in different regions. Therefore, the eligibility criteria for home visits are under consideration to integrate them with the implementation of a new annual vacation system. Along with the fast development of labour market, employees may select their jobs in a suitable working place. Therefore, the home visit system is becoming seldom used.

C. Marriage Leave, Bereavement Leave or Maternity Leave

159. According to Article 51 of the Labour Act, wages must be paid for statutory holidays, taking leave for weddings, funerals or to participate in social activities in accordance with the law.

160. Employees are entitled at least to three days' marriage leave. In the case of late marriage, i.e. marriage after the age of 23 (for women) and 25 (for men), 10–30 days would be added, prior to the amendment to the Population and Family Planning Law of PRC (effective 1 January 2016). After that date late marriage stipulations are no longer valid.

161. Normally, one to three days are given to close relatives of the deceased for attending the funeral.

162. Similar to the change of marriage leave, according to the Amendments to the Population and Family Planning Law of PRC, additional 30 days leave has been granted to all female employees for childbirth (in addition to 98 days childbirth). For a difficult childbirth, an extra 15 days' leave is granted. For multiple births, an extra 15 days leave for each additional baby born must be given. In case of a miscarriage, extra leave can be given according to medical advice.

D. Social Activities

163. Participating in social activities during working hours is deemed to be the equivalent of time spent as working time and is paid accordingly. The term 'social activities' in the context of the Chinese political and social system has a very broad meaning, including, for example, time spent promoting family planning, regular political study, people's militia training and attending meetings of various kinds, all of which could be seen as lawful participation in social activities. Article 10 of the Payment of Wages Tentative Provisions of 1994[41] defines the scope of the social activities as including:

– exercising the lawful right to vote or stand for election;

41. See China Update: the PRC, *Labour Law* (Asia Law and Practice 1995), at p. 111.

- when elected as a representative: to attend meetings convened by organizations such as the government at county (town) or district level or above, political parties, trade unions, the Communist Youth League, or the Women's Federation;
- acting as a witness at a people's court;
- attending a model worker or advanced workers meeting;
- as a member of the trade union committee at grass root level participating in trade union activities, according to trade union law; and
- other social activities which can be participated in lawfully.

IV. Educational Leave

164. From 1982 to 1992 numerous regulations and measures were adopted as constitutional provisions regarding the building up of a 'socialist nation with high material and spiritual civilization'. In socialist China, receiving education is not only regarded as a right but also as a duty of citizens (Art. 46 of the Constitution). In order to raise the scientific and cultural level of the whole nation, the state undertakes the development of socialist education at work. The 1982 Constitution particularly stipulates that the state will develop educational facilities in order to eliminate illiteracy and provide political, scientific, technical and professional education as well as general education for workers, peasants, state functionaries and other working people (Art. 19).

165. With a view to improving the educational attainment and professional competence of the workforce throughout the country, the State Council and the Central Committee of the Communist Party in 1981 issued the Decisions on Strengthening Work to Educate Employees[42] calling for the improvement of political education, comprehensive education, as well as vocational and technical education. The same issue was regulated again by the then Ministry of Labour in 1992.[43] Article 68 of the Labour Act addresses that provisions shall be made to cover the expenses of staff training. Nevertheless, only time for most on-the-job training is counted as working time, on average of a couple of days per year per head. It is at the discretion of the employer to grant additional educational leave for other career development courses.

166. Different categories of personnel have been participating in various training or educational programmes at multiple levels through different forms of educational undertakings. Full-time or part-time education can be granted as long as the normal operation of the work is not affected. In the 1980s, some people were sent to study for three to four years in college or at a university, while the employment relationship still remained. They were paid during their study, but obliged to return to the original employer upon completion of their studies. On some occasions, short-term educational leave is granted as an alternative arrangement for a redundant work force in the 1990s. The 1996 Vocational Education Law has made an

42. See *Complete Book of China's Labour Law* (Xinhua 1994), at p. 824.
43. *Ibid.*, at pp. 854 and 855.

effort to standardize the various practices of vocational education system in China so that the legal protection of the right to receiving education is enshrined in a consistent manner in both the 1986 Education Law (revised in 2006) and the 1996 Vocational Education Law.

Chapter 4. Remuneration

§1. Wage Reform and the Concept of Total Wages and Wage Level

I. Wage Reform

167. From the 1950s through to the 1960s to the 1970s, Chinese policy gave priority to production over living standards. A material incentive was rejected as it was considered to be against proletarian moral principles. A maximum amount of savings was encouraged while consumption was suppressed in order to support the principal position of heavy industry. Since the end of the 1970s, reform politics have gradually changed the long stagnation in real wage increases. Emphasis has been placed upon the Marxist teaching of the socialist distribution principle, i.e. 'distribution according to work' in combination with Deng Xiaoping's policy of material incentives in the form of wage increases. However, an improvement of living standards and an increase of the level of consumption have been accompanied by problems of price inflation which has been climbing from the mid-1980s to its peak of 21.7 per cent in 1994, which substantially affected real-wage increases. As compensation, different forms of bonuses and living subsidies have been distributed to maintain living standards and sustain a real wage increase. It is not until 1999 that China adopted Provisions on Protection for Minimum Living of Urban Residence. In 2007, the State Council issued its Notice for Establishment of the Minimum Living Security in Countryside, according to which China is for the first time to cover the security for minimum living standard to the rural areas.

168. Developed in the 1950s, wage standards have been ranked by different grades which indicate the wage-earner's status in the system. They differentiate according to the geographic place of employment and type of work. From 1956 to 1983, upgrading the wage level of employees was arranged by the state on a national basis. Since 1984, enterprises have been granted autonomy to arrange their employees' wage increases under the state unified policy. In 1984, enterprises were authorized to distribute bonuses, the amount of which in fact exceeded the total amount of the basic wage, together with payments for years of continuous service. In 1985 the State Council's Notice on Issues of Wage Reform in State Enterprises[44] further confirmed that enterprises have autonomy to use their 'wage increase fund' accumulated by themselves after implementing the 'system of linking enterprises' total wage amount with economic profit making. The state claimed that it would not arrange unified wage adjustments or wage increases for enterprises' employees according to the State Council's Notice on Issues of Wage Reform in State Enterprises of 1985. Unfortunately, it was common practice that profit-making enterprises, at their own discretion, distributed various bonuses and allowances in cash or in kind, evading either enterprise or individual income taxation, and this consequently led to unhealthy competition between enterprises. Regarding state macro-control over the national payroll, this basically includes systems of linking the total

44. See *Complete Book of China's Labour Law* (Xinhua 1994), at p. 228.

wage to economic efficiency system (Ministry of Labour, 1997 the Tentative Measures for Implementing Wage Guideline System in Pilot Regions), wage guideline system and the labour market price level guidance system (Ministry of Labour and Social Security, 1999 Notice on Establishing the Labour Market Price Level Guidance System).

The Wage Guideline System is made with reference to the regional economic growth rate, productivity, CPI and in consideration of other factors such as the local employment status, labour market price and labour cost. It gives benchmark, maximum and minimum of the annual wage increase rate. On the other hand, the labour market price level guidance gives market information of the pay levels and prices in different regions, industries and jobs based on statistics collected from various sources in scientific, standardized market survey and analysis.

169. On the other hand, state macro-regulation plays a crucial role. It is directly responsible for salary adjustments or salary increases for staff in state organs and institutions. A system of staff salary increases, based on professional post and grade, was planned and implemented in 1993.[45] In addition, the state has power to exercise its macro-regulation and control of the national wage scale and labour costs. Related to this, the concept of the total wage was defined and regulated by the State Statistic Bureau in 1990 and approved by the State Council[46] in order to standardize the calculation of total wages and to facilitate the formation and examination of wage plans. In accordance with the Regulations on Minimum Wages in Enterprises of 1993 (replaced by the Regulations on Minimum Wages of 2004),[47] the machinery of fixing minimum wage rates was implemented at provincial level and supervised by the national authority as part of a drive to develop a market economy in which fair competition between enterprises and basic needs of employees and their families are taken into account. Furthermore, the concept of state statutory social insurance was established in the Labour Act of 1994.

170. The change of the low-wage system together with the reform of the labour insurance system to reduce enterprises' burdens of huge housing subsidies, medical care and other insurance benefits led to the transformation of the pattern of state control in this regard. To relieve the constraints of state budgets with respect to a national wage scale and labour costs (including insurance and allowances, etc.), wage reform and labour insurance reform make it possible to encourage initiatives, to some extent, from regional or local levels. In accordance with the 1993 Opinion on Strengthening the Macro-Regulation of Enterprises' Total Wages, issued by the then Ministry of Labour, the so-called flexible wage plan has been adopted, under which three methods of regulation and control of labour-wages are to be applied. In most state enterprises, the linking of economic profits to the total wage plan applies. To those enterprises which have not yet implemented the system of linking the economic profits to the total wage plan, but are still making profits, the fixed total wage

45. See *Complete Book of China's Labour Law* (Xinhuan 1994), at p. 228.
46. See Composition of Total Wages Provisions in *International Encyclopaedia of Labour Law and Industrial Relations* (Legislation) PR China, p. 43.
47. *Ibid.* at p. 88.

applies, regardless of increases or decreases in personnel. To the remaining enterprises the state-planned wage scale and wage quota still apply.[48] The five factors for determining and adjusting the local minimum wage are the minimum living expenses of a worker and the minimum average living expenses of his dependants, the average social wage level, labour productivity, employment situation and difference in levels of economic development between the different regions. The minimum wage does not include overtime pay, shift (middle and night shift) and high/low temperature allowance, allowance for jobs with hazard and poison risks, insurance and benefits and non-monetary payments such as meal, housing etc. As stated by the Human Rights Implementation and Assessment Report (2012–2015), in the period 2012–2015, 25, 27, 19 and 27 regions adjusted the minimum wages at the rates of 20.1 per cent, 17.0 per cent, 14.1 per cent and 14.9 per cent respectively, with the target to increase the minimum wage to 40 per cent of the social average wage.

II. The Concept of Total Wages and Wage Levels

171. State control of national wage scales and of labour costs through the planning and allocation of labour-wage budget quotas to state and public sectors is still the core part of the Chinese remuneration system in the state-owned sector. Against this background, the total wage concept has to be adopted by employing units for the purpose of state supervision of statistics. The total wage refers to the total amount of remuneration for labour, paid directly by each unit to all of its employees during a particular period, in accordance with Article 2 of the Composition of the Total Wages Provisions of 1990. It specifies the composition of total wages as the following six elements:

(i) time wage (which refers to remuneration paid, based on time wage rates (including regional subsidies for the cost of living) and the time worked);
(ii) piece wage (which refers to remuneration paid based on unit price for work done);
(iii) bonuses (which refer to extra payments made for increase of revenue or reduction of expenditure);
(iv) allowances and subsidies (which refer to allowances paid in consideration of special or extra efforts or for other special reasons, as well as commodity price subsidies paid in order to ensure that the level of wages are not affected by changes in commodity prices);
(v) overtime pay (which refers to payment for extra shifts or extra hours); and
(vi) wages paid due to special circumstances.

Employer's expenditure used for labour protection, social insurance and staff benefits, travel and meal allowances and severance payments is not counted as part of

48. See *Complete Book of China's Labour Law* (Xinhua 1994), at p. 293; some other regulations concerning total wage administration can be found at pp. 283 and 285.

the total wages. Importantly, the reference base for the social insurance contributions is the total wage, not the basic wage. The employer must calculate each and every employee's total annual wages once a year for adjustment of social insurance contributions.

172. The wage level refers to the level of the average wage of employees in a certain locality within a certain period. The second paragraph of Article 46 of the Labour Act sets out the principle of raising the wage level base on economic development while the state exercises macro-regulation and control over the total wages. Article 47 of the Labour Act vests in the employer the power of determining the wage level independently, in compliance with the law and based on business and economic results. As China considers itself a developing country, wage increases are required to follow two principles, namely, the increase of the rate of average wage levels must not exceed the increase of the rate of social labour productivity; the increase of the rate of total wages must not exceed the increase of the rate of national income.

173. In line with the Notice on the Wage Reform covering Staff and Personnel Working in State Agent and Institutions issued by the State Council Oct. 1993, the development of a system of salary standards for staff in state organs and institutions, taking into consideration professional posts and grades, tends to be separate from the wage system for industrial workers. The composition of the staff salary includes:

(i) professional post salaries ranging from three to eight levels, depending on the duties involved;
(ii) grade salary with fifteen levels, depending on experience and ability;
(iii) basic salary with a fixed amount of 90 yuan to every member of staff; and
(iv) payment for length of service.

174. Since the middle of the 1980s, wages have consisted of the basic wage, payment for years of continuous service, position-related wages and incentive wages for workers in enterprises. The system of time wages, piece wages, and post wages may serve as the main calculation measure, supplemented by incentive wages (including production bonuses, saving bonuses, labour competition bonuses and other forms of bonus) and allowances and living subsidies. Due to the complexity of a position-related wage involving different types of job positions in different industries or sectors, the detailed classification of types of jobs was indexed by the then Ministry of Labour as of the end of 1992 and published ever since. In May 1999, China published its Code for Classification of Professionals. The latest improved version of the Code was made in 2015. With the development of the market economy, China will update its standards for job and professional classifications from time to time.

III. Determination of Wage Distribution and Wage Payment

175. Determination of wage distribution follows the principles of distribution according to work and equal pay for equal work. In addition, minimum wages are guaranteed.

176. The principles and practices of the determination of wage distribution intend to dismantle the 'iron wage system' of guaranteed wage payments regardless of a worker's actual production, and the 'iron armchair system' of the communist cadres receiving guaranteed positions regardless of performance. Both individual performances and the enterprise's profits are taken into consideration when determining an increase of wages for an enterprise worker. In accordance with the Labour Act, wage increases are based on economic development; employers, in accordance with the characteristics of their production and business operations and their economic results, independently determine their own wage distribution measures and wage levels.

177. Wage payment refers to items of payments, wage payment levels, methods of payments, recipient of payments, time of payments and payments in special circumstances according to the Payment of Wages Tentative Provisions of 1994[49] and its supplementary rules of 1995.

178. Wages must be paid in legal tender. Material goods and valuable securities may not be substituted for payment in legal tender. Normally the payment is handed over directly to the employees concerned. Some employers appoint banks to distribute wages either through bank account transfers, or they pay cash directly to the employees concerned. When employees are absent with justification, their relatives or other appointed persons may collect the wages on their behalf. Employers are requested to keep the wage payment list including wage amount, payment date, recipient's name and signature for at least two years.

179. Dates of payment can be agreed upon by the employer and employee. Advance payments on the nearest working day must be made if such an agreed date of payment falls on a holiday or rest day, the payment should be effected in advance on the workday closest to the payday. For an employee involved in one course of temporary work or one specific job, the employer must pay the wage on completion of that work by the employee, in accordance with the provisions of the relevant agreement and contract. When a labour contract is terminated in accordance with the law, the wages must be paid in a lump sum upon the termination of the contract.

180. A written record must be kept regarding the amount of the payment, time of the payment, name and recipient of the wages paid. Employers are required to provide individual employees with a copy of a wage slip with all the necessary information regarding payment. With acceptance of electronic data, the bank transfer record may satisfy all such procedures.

---

49. See China Update: the PRC, *Labour Law* (Asia Law & Practice 1995), at p. 111.

§2. MINIMUM WAGES

I. Principles and Standards

181. When the wages reform destroyed the 'iron wage system', there was no measure to prevent enterprises, especially in the private sector, from underpaying their employees, and this also resulted in unfair competition between enterprises. Learning from international experience, the concepts of a minimum wage and a minimum standard of living were introduced to China in 1993. The development of labour law in setting up minimum standards is a benefit from China's gradual acceptance of the socialist market philosophy and the practice of international labour standards. The minimum wage refers to the minimum labour remuneration that the employer must pay according to law when the labourer provides normal labour within the working time stipulated in the legal working time or a signed labour contract.

182. Regulations on Minimum Wages in Enterprises were issued by the former Ministry of Labour, effective as of 24 November 1993, which was replaced by the newly promulgated Regulations on Minimum Wages in Enterprises effective as of 1 March 2004. All types of enterprise are required to follow the minimum wage rate fixed by the government at provincial level. This minimum wage rate is adjusted at least once every two years. The regulations were formulated in line with principles of social equality and fair competition, improving and ensuring living standards along with levels of economic development. It is required that the minimum wage rate be set up on a monthly basis, or it may be on an hourly basis, excluding payment for overtime, swing or night shifts, work in toxic or high/low temperature working environments, as well as social insurance and other welfare benefits for workers. In consideration of different levels of development in different localities and sectors, minimum wage rates may be varied in the same region; therefore, the regulations have not directly set up national minimum wage rates.

183. Several internationally accepted methods for the calculation of minimum wage rates are appended to the 2004 Regulations on Minimum Wages. In setting and adjusting the minimum wage rates, the following factors have to be taken into account:

(i) the average living cost for urban residents;
(ii) contributions to social security funds and housing fund by the individual employee;
(iii) minimum wages standard of the working force;
(iv) the unemployment rate;
(v) the level of economic development; and
(vi) an adjustment factor.

II. Minimum Wage Fixing Machinery

184. Tripartitism is adopted in the minimum wage fixing machinery under the Regulations on Minimum Wages, though this is not explicitly provided for by the Labour Act. The national labour authority exercises unified supervision over the national minimum wage system with the consultation of the All-China Federation of Trade Unions (ACFTU) and China Enterprise Directors' Association (CEDA)/ China Enterprises Association (CEA), while the local labour authority at provincial level is in charge of the administration of the minimum wage system in its region. In fixing a minimum wage, the local labour authority at provincial level has to work together with the trade union and the employer organization at the corresponding level, as required by Article 8 of the Regulations on Minimum Wages. The provincial minimum wage rate or its adjustment shall be endorsed by the national labour authority in consultation with the ACFTU and the CEDA/ CEA. In this way a tripartite system is applied.

185. Enterprises must inform their employees about the relevant provisions on minimum wages. The minimum wage rates and adjustments of them are required to be made public. Government and trade union inspection and supervision of the application of minimum wages are further provided for in the Regulations on Minimum Wages. In violation of the minimum wage rate, an employer may be liable to pay the infringed employee a compensation for one to five times of the wages owed to the employee.

§3. Protective Measures and Liability

I. Deduction

186. Protective provisions can be found in the Payment of Wages Tentative Provisions. Deductions from an employee's remuneration are limited to individual income tax deduction, social security premium deduction, child support and maintenance fees, which are required to be deducted by a court decision, and other regulated deductions. Where losses are suffered by an employing unit caused by an employee who is liable to pay compensation, the compensation may be deducted from the wage of the employee concerned in accordance with 1994 Provisional Regulation on Wage Payment. However, such a deduction will not exceed 20 per cent of the monthly wage. If the amount of the remaining wages after the deduction is less than the local minimum wage, payment must be made in accordance with the minimum wage standard. The employer shall pay the wages of the laborer according to the standard stipulated in the labour contract during one wage payment term (normally one month) in which suspension of the production is not due to the reason caused by employee. In practice, if suspension of production or work lasts more than one month, the employer and employee may make mutual consensus on rest days for employee with less payment during such rest days.

II. Severance Payments

187. See discussion below in Chapter 6.

III. Overtime Payment

188. Overtime payment is of a protective nature set out in the Payment of Wages Tentative Provisions which repeat Article 44 of the Labour Act. Remuneration of no less than 150 per cent of the wage shall be paid to the employee for extended working hours on weekdays. Remuneration of no less than 200 per cent of the wage must be paid if the extended hours are arranged on a rest day and no deferred rest day can be arranged. If the extended hours are arranged on a statutory holiday, remuneration of no less than 300 per cent of the wage must be paid. However, the maximum overtime must not exceed 36 hours per month.

IV. Priority of Repayment to Employees by Bankrupt Enterprises

189. Wages owed to employees by a bankrupt enterprise are required to be paid as a priority in the discharge order according to Article 37 of the Law of the People's Republic of China on Enterprise Bankruptcy (Trial Implementation) of 1986[50] (which is replaced by the Insolvency Law of 2007).

V. Liability

190. Under Article 91 of the Labour Act those employers who:

(i) deduct or unreasonably delay payment;
(ii) refuse to pay for overtime work;
(iii) pay below the local minimum wage rate; and
(iv) refuse to pay the severance payment;

will be liable for compensation for the economic loss of the employee concerned.

191. In accordance with Article 85 of the Labour Contract Law, if an employer is in any of the following situations, the labour administration authority shall order the employer to pay the remuneration, overtime pay or severance pay within a specified period of time; if the remuneration is lower than the local minimum wage rate, the employer must pay the difference; if payment is not made within the time limit, the labour administration authority shall order the employer pay damages additionally to the employee at a rate of not less than 50 per cent and not more than 100 per cent of the amount payable:

50. See *The Laws of the People's Republic of China 1983–1986* (Foreign Languages Press Beijing 1987), at p. 289.

(a) fails to pay an employee his/her remuneration in full and on time as stipulated in his/her labour contract or prescribed by the state;
(b) pays remuneration below the local minimum wage rate;
(c) arranges overtime work without paying overtime pay; or
(d) rescinds or terminates a labour contract without paying the employee severance pay pursuant to this Law.

Chapter 5. Job Security

192. Before the establishment of the labour market and the comprehensive social security scheme, there was no legal concept of job security in China, because state enterprises looked after workers on behalf of the state. Under the planned economy system, the main characteristic of urban employment policy was to implement mandatory labour plans: the government took over a unified administrative assignment and contracting system in order to have workers permanently employed. Officially there was no redundancy and unemployment. The approach to job security was a matter of state interest. In the 1990s, labour legislation transformed paternalistic job security to a market-oriented system. The Employment Promotion Law of the PRC, promulgated on 30 August 2007 and modified in 2015, covers topics on policy support, equal employment, employment service, management and assistance, vocational education and training, as well as supervision, inspection and liability. Employers' liability for maintaining jobs for employees and state statutory provisions to maintain employees' rights to access the social security scheme during and after the term of their labour contracts, are the key aspects to making the termination of individual labour contracts possible both in law and in practice. This legal approach to job security is not merely in consideration of state interest, as it also concerns the individual's legitimate rights in line with the principle of social solidarity.

§1. Redundancy and Reduction

193. The substantial redundancy and reduction in the field of coal, textile, machinery and other industrial sectors owned by the state took place in the 1990s. Tens of millions of state-owned workers became unemployed, forming a 'laid-off tide'. Included in the estimation of the number of surplus workers are those who have no job assignments and are awaiting resettlement in enterprises and are regarded as redundant workers in China. They are mainly employed in the textile, light chemical and mechanical industries. The majority are middle-aged and a large number of them are women. The 1993 Regulations concerning the Arrangement of Redundancy in State-Owned Enterprises were adopted according to which issues of redundancy were to be handled in a prescribed way (see above, Chapter 2, §3).

194. The resettlement of redundant workers relies mainly on enterprises themselves with supplementary social support. Due to a preferential governmental policy regarding tax exemption, enterprises normally set up a company in tertiary industry (i.e. in the service sector) to resettle part of their redundant workers. Training is also provided for a possible new job assignment created in their own enterprises or in other enterprises. The employer may also 'export the service' of these redundant workers while still retaining their membership so as to cover their living subsidies and social insurance benefits when they work for other employers.

195. The 1994 Regulations concerning the Reduction of Personnel for Economic Reasons in Enterprises[51] were adopted by the former Ministry of Labour to implement the Labour Act provisions regarding employers' rights to reduce the number of their personnel due to the employer being in serious economic difficulties. Article 27 of the Labour Act provides that when a reduction of personnel is really necessary during a period of statutory restructuring, if an enterprise is on the verge of bankruptcy or if an enterprise runs into difficulties in production and management, such reduction can be made after the situations have been explained to a trade union or employees 30 days in advance, and opinions have been solicited from them and a report has been submitted to the labour administration department. Further restrictive rules are found in the Labour Contract Law (Art. 41) according to which reduction of more than 20 employees or more than 10 per cent of the work force in specified circumstances will be subject to the legal procedures provided in Article 27 of the Labour Act.

196. The 1994 Regulations concerning the Reduction of Personnel for Economic Reasons in Enterprises provide further procedures for reductions which ensure that employees or trade unions and the government have been sufficiently consulted. A period of 30 days' notice to trade unions or employees is required, a reduction proposal must be submitted which includes the names of the employees to be made redundant and a schedule for implementing the reduction and the methods for economic compensation for employees made redundant; then the proposal shall be revised and improved based on opinions of trade unions and employees. Employers are required to reconsider the reduction if it is viewed by trade unions or employees to be against the laws and/or regulations and/or collective agreements. The proposal with the trade unions' and employees' opinion shall be submitted to the labour administration department for its opinion before it is formally announced. Procedures for cancellation of the labour contracts will then be dealt with. Economic compensation shall be paid at an amount equal to one month's wages for every full year of work, based on the average monthly wage of the employing unit. In addition, the unemployed, as a result of such a reduction, may register with a local labour employment service organization and apply for unemployment relief. Article 41 of the Labour Contract Law requires that when reducing the workforce, the employer shall retain the following persons with priority:

(a) those who have concluded with the employer fixed-term employment contracts with a relatively long term;
(b) those who have concluded open-ended employment contracts with the employer; or
(c) those who are the only ones in their families to be employed and whose families have elderly persons or minors for whom they need to support and maintain.

51. See China Update: the PRC, *Labour Law* (Asia Law & Practice 1995), at p. 118.

Furthermore, if an employer that has reduced its workforce hires people again within six months, it must notify the persons laid off and recruit them on a preferential basis.

§2. Restriction for Termination of the Employment Relationship

197. Article 5 of the 1994 Regulations concerning the Reduction of Personnel for Economic Reasons in Enterprises prohibits employers from reducing those employees who are confirmed to have totally or partially lost the ability to work due to occupational diseases or injuries suffered at work; those who are within the stipulated period of medical treatment for illness or injury; those female workers who are pregnant, or in a puerperal or breast-feeding period; or those who are in another situation stipulated by the laws and regulations. The Ministry of Human Resources and Social Security promulgated a draft of new Regulations on Personnel Reduction in Enterprises in 2014 to solicit public opinion. These new regulations have not been finally issued.

198. Under Article 26 of the Labour Act and Article 40 of the Labour Contract law, the employer may terminate the employment relationship where an employee is unable to do his original work or any new work arranged by the employing unit after the completion of medical treatment for illness or injury not suffered at work, or when an employee is unqualified for his work and remains unqualified even after receiving training or after being transferred to another post. Where a major change in the objective circumstances under which the contract was concluded has resulted in the contract being unable to be performed and the parties have failed to reach an agreement on the modification of such a contract after consultation and discussion, the contract can also be terminated by the employer. Notwithstanding Article 26 of the Labour Act and Article 40 (no-fault termination) and 41 (economic lay off) of the Labour Contract Law, an employer cannot terminate the employment relationship if an employee (a) who has been engaged in work exposed to occupational hazards has not undergone a post-employment occupational health check or during a period where an employee is suspected of having an occupational illness or under medical observation; (b) who is confirmed to have totally or partially lost the ability to work due to occupational diseases or injuries suffered at work; (c) who is within the stipulated period of medical treatment for illness or injury; (d) who is pregnant, in a puerperal or breast-feeding period; (e) who has been employed by the same enterprise for more than 15 years and less than 5 years from the official retirement age; (f) who is in any other situation stipulated by the laws and regulations.

199. The medical treatment period is defined in the 1994 Provisions on the Period of Medical Treatment for Enterprise Employees Who Fall Ill or Who Are Injured Off Duty.[52] It refers to the time when an employee, due to illness or injury suffered off duty, ceases to work in order to rest and recuperate, without termination of his labour contract. The length of such medical treatment period can be from

52. See China Update: the PRC, *Labour Law* (Asia Law & Practice Ltd 1995), at p. 121.

three months to two years depending on the seniority of the employee. The calculation methods for medical treatment period vary from region to region. It has recently been found difficult to restrict the situation where an employee travels as a tourist during the medical treatment period. It is also sometimes hard to calculate the medical treatment period.

§3. Re-employment Projects and the Social Insurance Scheme for the Unemployed

200. Strictly speaking, unemployment insurance is not a question of job security. But in the context of Chinese labour reform, job security, re-employment projects and unemployment insurance are an integrated effort to enhance harmonious relationships between the individual, the employer and society. The employers still play a significant role in relation to governmental re-employment projects and unemployment insurance schemes, while society (*die Gesellschaft*) is still developing towards a more independent and self-sufficient handling of labour issues. It used to be the long-term objective that China wanted to set up an obligatory unemployment insurance system covering all employees, with contributions shared between employers and employees, and with combinations of unemployment benefit and measures for re-employment.

201. The 1986 Regulations on Unemployment Insurance for the Employees of State-owned Enterprises (replaced by the 1993 Regulations on Unemployment Insurance for the Employees of the State-owned Enterprises) have been adopted, when the labour contract system and Bankruptcy Law were introduced. The 1993 Regulations on Unemployment Insurance for the Employees of the State-owned Enterprises have been implemented based on the then Ministry of Labour's Directives of Implementation of the Regulations. However, the 1993 Regulations apply only to workers and employees of state-owned enterprises. The Regulations on Unemployment Insurance of 1999, superseded the 1993 Regulations on Unemployment Insurance for the Employees of the State-owned Enterprises, are to cover all employees working in enterprises regardless of the ownership nature of enterprises. Statutory unemployment insurance scheme was integrated in the Social Insurance Law in 2010 with the unemployment insurance stipulations covering all employees uniformly.

202. Some provinces such as Shangdong, Hubei, Zhijian, Fujian, Anhui, Hainan, Shanghai, Tianjing had their own provisional rules, which provide an unemployment insurance scheme not only for employees of state-owned enterprises but also for collectives, foreign investment enterprises and private enterprises. The 1993 Regulations on Unemployment Insurance for Employees of State-owned Enterprises were replaced by the 1999 Regulations on Unemployment Insurance[53] according to which unemployment insurance covers employees in state-owned

53. See *International Encyclopaedia for Labour Law and Industrial Relations* [Legislation] PR China, p. 146.

enterprises, urban collective enterprises, foreign-investment enterprises and urban private enterprises. Article 6 of the 1999 Regulations on Unemployment Insurance expressly stipulates that for urban enterprises, contributions to unemployment insurance shall be made by both individual workers and employers, but for contracted peasant workers only the employer should make contributions and no individual payment is needed. If these contracted peasant workers do not have a labour contract extended or their labour contract is prematurely terminated, they may get a one-off life allowance from the social insurance agency, providing they have worked continuously for one year or longer.

203. In 1991, Hanzhou, Shanghai, Dalian and Guangzhou were chosen by the then Ministry of Labour to extend the scope of eligibility for unemployment benefits, which under the 1986 Regulations were only available to those laid off due to bankruptcy or a major restructuring of enterprises on the verge of bankruptcy, to those dismissed because of a disciplinary offence or to contract workers on the expiration of their contracts, and to those that were redundant because their enterprise stopped production and was undergoing reorganization. If employees lost their job for one of the statutory reasons and registered with an unemployment insurance institute (Labour Service Centre) under the labour administration, they were entitled to unemployment benefits. The unemployment security of the peasant workers is much lower than the urban workers.

204. The duration of entitlement to unemployment relief is dependent on the number of years of service during which insurance premiums are paid. Those who have worked for more than one year, but for less than five years, before becoming unemployed, may receive a maximum of 12 months' unemployment relief. When an unemployed person is re-employed and then becomes unemployed again, the period of unemployment insurance entitlement shall be accumulated and not exceed 24 months. Those who worked for more than five years, but for less than ten years, before becoming unemployed, may receive a maximum of 18 months' unemployment relief. Those who worked for ten years or more, before becoming unemployed, may receive 24 months' unemployment relief. Entitlement to unemployment insurance benefit terminates upon expiry of the maximum period for unemployment relief, when the unemployed person finds new job, joins the army or resides abroad, or refuses without proper justification introductions to a new job provided by an authority or organization designated by local government, is entitled to a pension, is sent for labour re-education or commits a crime during the period of receiving unemployment relief.

205. Statistics indicated in China's *Labour Security Development Report 2016* show that by the end of 2015, China had 774 million employees in total, with 173 million unemployment insurance participants. In the Job Promotion Programme within the 13th Five-Year Plan for Economic and Social Development of the People's Republic of China (from 2016 to 2020) issued by the State Council, China aims to achieve the following objectives by 2020: the increase of the newly hired urban employees will be more than 50 million; the registered unemployment rate shall be controlled below 5 per cent; the employment situation of key groups including university graduates and migrant workers shall be basically stable; the labour contract signing rate shall be above 90 per cent.

206. The former Ministry of Labour launched a pilot re-employment project in the cities with serious unemployment problems at the end of 1993. The project had been carried out nationwide since 1995. Numerous measures have been adopted, including subsidizing newly established enterprises to recruit the unemployed. The unemployed are also encouraged to set up a privately run business or engage in self-employment with settlement allowances or a relief fund. For resettlement of redundant workers (see above, §1).

Chapter 6. The Termination of the Individual Labour Contract

§1. General Methods of Terminating the Individual Labour Contract

I. Expiry and Termination

207. Chinese labour law defines the difference between termination upon expiry of a labour contract or upon termination arising out of a condition agreed upon by the parties and termination of a labour contract on statutory grounds or mutual agreement. The legal regulation of termination of the individual labour contract is intended to ensure both the employer's autonomy in the employment of personnel, and the individual's right to choose and quit his or her job.

208. Termination of a labour contract on mutual agreement means mutual consent has been reached with regard to termination of the labour contract (*see* Art. 24 of the Labour Act and Article 36 of the Labour Contract Law). Termination on statutory grounds means that the contract is rightfully terminated by one party without obtaining of the consent from the other party due to statutory reasons.

209. There are four circumstances under which termination of a labour contract is mentioned in the Labour Act, i.e. termination based on mutual agreement (Art. 24); termination by the employer with 30 days' notice (Arts. 26 and 27); termination by the employer without 30 days' notice (Art. 25); and termination by the employee with or without 30 days' notice (Arts. 31 and 32 respectively).

II. Termination by the Employer without 30 Days' Written Notice

210. In accordance with Article 25 of the Labour Act and Article 39 of the Labour Contract Law, the employer may terminate the labour contract in any one of the following circumstances:

(i) if the employee proves to be unqualified during the probationary period;
(ii) if the employee seriously contravenes labour discipline or the employee unit's rules and regulations;
(iii) if the employee seriously derelicts his duty and engages in malpractice for selfish ends, causing substantial loss to the employing unit's interests;
(iv) if the employee has concurrently established a labour relationship with another employer, which materially affects the completion of his/her tasks with the first-mentioned employer, or he refuses to rectify the matter after the employer brought the same to his/her attention;
(v) if the labour contract is rendered void due to its conclusion by use of fraudulent or coercive tactics or taking advantage of the counterparty's unfavourable position to cause the counterparty to act against the real intention;
(vi) if the employee is investigated and determined to be criminally responsible in accordance with the law.

211. All the above listed circumstances involve termination of the labour contract by the employer without requirement for prior notice due to the fault of the employee under Article 25 of the Labour Act and Article 39 of the labour Contract Law. Article 30 of the Labour Act, however, allows the trade unions to make representations on behalf of an employee. Article 43 of the Labour Contract Law further stipulates that when an employer is to rescind a labour contract unilaterally, the employer shall notify the labour union the reason therefore in advance. If the employer violates laws, administrative regulations or the labour contract, the labour union is entitled to request that the employer to rectify such matter. The employer shall study the labour union's opinions and notify the labour union in writing as to the outcome of its handling of the matter.

III. Termination by the Employer with 30 Days' Written Notice

212. Under Article 26 of the Labour Act and Article 40 of the Labour Contract Law, the employer may terminate the labour contract with 30 days' prior notice in any one of the following circumstances:

(i) where an employee is unable to do his original work or any new work arranged by the employing unit after the completion of medical treatment for illness or injury not suffered at work;
(ii) when an employee is unqualified for his work and remains unqualified even after receiving training or being transferred to another post;
(iii) where a major change in the objective circumstances under which the contract was concluded has resulted in the contract being unable to be carried out and the parties have failed to reach an agreement on the modification of such a contract after consultation and discussion.

213. In accordance with Article 27 of the Labour Act and Article 41 of the Labour Contract Law, termination of the labour contract due to redundancy is not only subject to 30 days' notice, but also to some other procedures (see above Chapter 5 §1). It is noticeable that employees in the following conditions are protected from being made redundant:

(i) employees who have engaged in work exposed to occupational hazards have not undergone post-employment occupational health check or during a period where an employee is suspected to have an occupational illness or under medical observation;
(ii) employees who are confirmed to have totally or partially lost the ability to work due to occupational diseases or work-related injuries;
(iii) employees who are within the stipulated period of medical treatment for illness or injury;
(iv) employees who are pregnant, or in a puerperal or breast-feeding period;
(v) employees who have been employed by the same enterprise for more than 15 years and less than 5 years from the official retirement age; or
(vi) employees who are in another situation stipulated by the laws and regulations.

214. In accordance with Article 29 of the Labour Act and Article 42 of the Labour Contract Law, termination of the contract with 30 days' notice and termination of the contract due to reduction of personnel are not applicable to those employees, engaging in the work exposing to occupational diseases hazards, who are not yet undergone the occupational health check for their departure of the job position or who are under the medical observation; those who are confirmed to have totally or partially lost the ability to work due to occupational diseases or injuries suffered at work; those who are within the stipulated period of medical treatment for illness or injury; those female workers who are pregnant, in a puerperal or breast-feeding period; or those who have continuously served for not less than fifteen years and less than five years away from statutory retirement age; or those who are in another situation stipulated by the laws and regulations.

IV. Termination by the Employee

215. During the probationary period, both parties to the labour contract are allowed to terminate the contract without 30 days' prior notice. However, an employee intending to terminate the labour contract during the probationary period shall give 3 days' notice. Otherwise, Article 31 of the Labour Act requires that the employee must give the employer 30 days' prior written notice of termination of the labour contract.

216. In accordance with Article 32 of the Labour Act, the 30-days' notice requirement for an employee does not apply in the following three situations:

(i) during the probationary period;
(ii) if the employer forces the employee to work by means of violence, threats, or illegal restrictions on personal freedom;
(iii) if the employer fails to pay wages or provide working conditions in accordance with the labour contract.

Article 38 of the Labour Contract Law provides additional situations under which the employee may terminate the labour contract without 30 days' prior notice:

(i) the employer fails to pay the social insurance premiums for the employee according to the law;
(ii) the employer has rules and regulations that violate laws or regulations, thereby damaging the employee's rights and interests;
(iii) the employer causes the labour contract to be null and void due to an employment agreement concluded by the employer's fraud, coercion or exploitation of other party's unfavourable position as specified in Article 26(1) of the Labour Contract Law;
(iv) the employer has other circumstances specified by laws or administrative regulations which permit a employee to rescind his/her labour contract.

§2. SEVERANCE PAY

217. Employees whose labour contracts are terminated by an employer with the employee's agreement; whose labour contracts are terminated with 30 days' notice; and whose labour contracts are terminated due to redundancy, are eligible for, or entitled to, severance pay under the 1994 Economic Compensation for Breach and Termination of Contracts Provision issued by the former Ministry of Labour.[54] As a part of the pro-employee labour codification movement, the Labour Contract Law imposes severance payment obligations on an employer under some additional circumstances where a labour contract is terminated. See below paragraph 224.

218. Upon termination of the labour contract by the employer with the agreement between the parties, the employer has to pay economic compensation equal to one month's wages for every full year of work, up to a maximum of 12 months according to the employment term of the employees.

219. The labour contract is terminated by the employer due to the employee's illness or injury, which did not occur at work, and if he is confirmed to be unable to perform his original work or any new work arranged by the employing unit after the statutory medical period, then the employer must pay economic compensation equal to one month's wages for every full year of work, according to the term of employment at the employing unit and at the same time must pay a minimum medical subsidy of six months' wages.

220. Upon termination of the labour contract by the employer due to the employee's incapacity to perform the job and remaining to be incapable after being trained or transferred to another job, the employee will be entitled to compensation equal to one month's wages for every full year of work up to a maximum of 12 months.

221. Those employees whose labour contract has been terminated by the employer due to a reduction of personnel or due to the change of the objective circumstances on which a labour contract has been concluded are entitled to compensation equal to one month's wages for every full year of work.

222. Upon implementation of the Labour Contract Law commenced from 1 January 2008, severance pay shall be also made by an employer to an employee under the circumstances where a labour contract is terminated unitarily by the employee without 30 days' notice due to statutory reasons (see paragraph 218 above); where a fixed-term labour contract is terminated upon expiration, unless the employee does not agree to renew the contract even though the conditions offered by the employer are the same as or better than those stipulated in the current contract; where termination of the labour contract is due to the employer's bankruptcy or the employer's business licence being revoked, the employer being ordered to close down, or the employer being earlier dissolved upon its decision. The Labour

54. See China Update: the PRC, *Labour Law* (Asia Law & Practice Ltd 1995), at p. 71.

Contract Law set the cap for calculating the severance pay, i.e. if monthly salary of the employee concerned is more than 300 per cent of the average monthly wage in the local city, the basis for the calculation of the severance payment payable shall be capped at three times the average monthly wages in the locality and shall be for not more than 12 years. In practice, in order to achieve the termination of the labour contract by mutual agreement, the severance payment would most probably exceed the cap.

In addition to the severance payments being paid in full, additional economic compensation equal to 50 to 100 per cent of the amount of such severance payments due shall be paid, if an employer fails to pay the severance payments to the employee concerned.

Chapter 7. Special Protection of Certain Categories of Workers, Protection against Discrimination in Employment

§1. Special Protection for Female Workers and Equality in Employment

223. China is very proud of its legal improvements in protecting women's rights in relation to work, politics, privacy, marriage, family, property and education. It hosted the International Women's Conference in 1995. Applicable regulations regarding the special protection of female workers at work emphasize the so-called 'five periods of protection' for female workers, namely protection during menstruation, protection during pregnancy, protection during childbirth, protection during the breast-feeding period and protection during the menopause. The Labour Act has also confirmed this practice. Nowadays, Chinese legislation is still striving to overcome the traditional legal assumption that women are physically and intellectually inferior to men. However, it is a social as well as a legal dilemma that providing special protection for female workers brings about the idea that women, by virtue of their gender, need special treatment, rather than equality. Further legal studies on discrimination in ten large cities were conducted by constitutional politics studies institute of China University of Political Science and Law in 2007 disclosed the unsatisfactory result in legal protection against employment discrimination in China. Violation of equal pay for equal work, prejudice over special categorized persons in employment were apparent according to the academic study (The Employment Discrimination in China: Current Conditions and Anti-Discrimination Strategies, 2007). It is found that the Labour Act failed to define employment discrimination and set no mechanism to provide remedies for the victims of discrimination. The basic concept of anti-discrimination recommended by the ILO Convention No. 111 seems to have immediate references to China. Scholars and social activists call for an Act against Employment Discrimination with emphasis on substantive equality. It is found that the employer's autonomy and the job seeker's right to equal employment are two opposing factors in practice. A 'merit-based approach' for recruitment is chosen to balance these two rights, which means that equal employment requires the employer to consider only the candidate's qualification and that candidates with equal qualifications shall be given the same opportunity of employment. However, a 'merit-based approach' cannot protect vulnerable groups such as female workers and disabled persons because the 'merit-based approach' may result in pursuit of maximum efficiency of economic profits which may cause a new kind of discrimination to such vulnerable groups. Thus, to protect these employees from discrimination, the employer must sacrifice some efficiency or take measures to eliminate the productivity gap. It is necessary to introduce a new kind of 'substantive equality' to make up the productivity disadvantage of these vulnerable groups and give them equal rights.

224. A government campaign to crack down on the abduction and sale of women and children over the years in 1980s raised general concern regarding the legal protection of women's rights, in 1992, the Law of the People's Republic of

China on the Protection of Rights and Interests of Women[55] was adopted and was deemed to be the first of its kind in the world.[56] This Law was modified in 2005 with emphasis on equal chances for women in receiving education, in employment, in social and political status. It is still ambiguous whether the legal protection of women is from the point of view of the protection of women's subjective rights or from the point of view of the protection of women as special objects in law. Nevertheless, Chapter IV of this Law specifically covers women's rights and interests relating to work by stressing the equal treatment in recruitment, pay, welfare benefits and allotment of housing; in addition, non-discrimination against women in promotion and entitlement to professional rank are provided for. Employing units are prohibited from dismissing female workers or unilaterally terminating a labour contract by reason of marriage, pregnancy, maternity leave or breast-feeding.

The State Council issued the 10-year Programme for the Development of Chinese Women (2001–2010) in May 2001 which demonstrated legal policy on protection of Chinese women in line with the Tenth Five-Year Plan for National Economic and Social Development of the People's Republic of China and Platform for Action adopted at the Fourth World Conference on Women. However, there is lack of final assessment on the implementation of the above-mentioned Chinese Programme for the Development of Chinese Women (2001–2010). An interim assessment report indicated that positive progress had been made while the shortcomings and recommendations for improvement were so limited that the programme could hardly serve as a guideline for legal policy change in protection for women at work. The similar Programme for the Development of Chinese Women (2011–2020) was promulgated in July 2011 with limited significance to guide and monitor the labour protection and equal treatment for women at work, because it is an idealistic presentation of perfection, instead of being systematic design for adjustment to the establishment taking into account pluralism in gender protection.

225. Both the Law on the Protection of Rights and Interests of Women and the Labour Act stress the principle of the equality of men and women in employment. In the recruitment of workers. Females must not be refused and nor must the standard be raised for women, except for posts or jobs unsuitable for women according to state provisions. In accordance with Article 57 of the Law on the Protection of Rights and Interests of Women, those who commit the following infringements upon a woman's lawful rights and interests relating to work will be ordered to make corrections and the responsible person may be subject to administrative sanctions for failure to deal with women's rights infringements and non-performance of the duties of the state agency and their personnel in stopping the infringement or providing assistance to the infringed woman. It is worth noticing that Chinese Civil Law and Labour Law stipulate harsh punishment for sexual harassment and domestic violence. The Rules for Implementation in Shanghai Municipality and in Jiangsu Municipality of the Law of Peoples Republic of China on Protection of Women's Rights and Interests state that no sexual harassment in the forms of language, words, image, telecommunication, physical act shall be conducted against a woman. It is

55. See *The Laws of the People's Republic of China 1990–1992* (Science Press, Beijing 1993), at p. 373.
56. See *China Daily*, 28 March 1992.

reported that in civil court cases, evidence of sexual harassment and domestic violence are provided by the plaintiff with a certain degree of difficulty. Sexual harassment at work in practice is often regulated in a labour manual subject to which either a female or male employee committed the act of sexual harassment would lead to termination of his/her employment contract.

§2. Special Protection for Juvenile Workers

226. The 1991 Law of the People's Republic of China on the Protection of Minors[57] governs those who are under the age of 18 (this accounts for one third of the Chinese population). This Law, modified in December 2006 and October 2012, emphasizes the protection of minors by the family, school, society and judicial organs. The second paragraph of Article 38 of this law explicitly states that no organization or individual may recruit minors under the age of 16, unless otherwise specified by the state. Any organization or individual that recruits, according to the relevant regulations of the state, juveniles over the age of 16 but under 18, must, in respect of the type of job, duration and intensity of labour as well as protective measures, follow the relevant provisions of the state and must not assign them to any over strenuous, poisonous or harmful labour or any dangerous operation.

227. Under the Labour Act, 'juvenile workers' refers to labourers who have reached 16 years of age but have not yet reached 18 years of age. The Labour Act states that juvenile workers shall not be arranged to work in mines and wells, carry out work of a hazardous or harmful nature, carry out work requiring Grade IV physical labour intensity as stipulated by the state or other work that shall be avoided (Art. 64). Employers are required by the Labour Act to conduct a physical examination of juvenile workers on a regular basis. State stipulations concerning the limitation on job positions for juvenile workers are found in the Rules on the Special Protection for Juvenile Workers of 1995.[58]

228. Article 94 of the Labour Act is consistent with Article 49 of the 1991 Law of the People's Republic of China on the Protection of Minors which imposes fines on or revocation of the business licence of those who illegally hire minors under the age of 16. Under the Provision of the Administrative Penalties for Violating the Labour Act, a fine of up to RMB 3,000 yuan may be imposed for violating the Labour Act provisions regarding special protection for juvenile workers.

57. See *The Laws of the People's Republic of China 1990–1992* (Science Press, Beijing 1993), at p. 289.
58. See *2009 Compilation of Laws and Regulations on the Labour and Human Resources of the PRC* (Law Press-China), at p. 233.

§3. Special Protection for and Promotion of Employment for the Handicapped

229. The employment of handicapped persons is subject to special provisions in China in accordance with Article 14 of the Labour Act. The 1991 Law of the People's Republic of China on the Protection of Disabled Persons[59] is formulated to promote the equal and full participation of the handicapped in education, employment and other spheres of social life while protecting their rights and interests. The state has to provide for disabled persons who are unable to earn a living, while promoting the social and occupational integration of those who are able to work. Chapter IV of this law deals with employment for the handicapped by specifying the right for the handicapped to work, government employment policy, employment method and support for employment for the handicapped. According to *Labour and Social Security in China* (White Paper), during 1996 to 2000, more than 1.1 million disabled persons were provided with skill training, and another 1.1 million found jobs.

230. Concentrated employment of the handicapped shall be provided in welfare enterprises for disabled persons, workers' sanatoria, massage therapy centres and other enterprises and institutions of a welfare nature. A proportion of the handicapped is required to be employed in appropriate types of jobs and posts in different sectors. Support measures include providing preferential tax treatment to welfare enterprises, assignment of jobs with a reserved quota to the handicapped, providing business chances and conditions for the handicapped. Non-discrimination against the handicapped in education and vocational and technical training are also specifically provided for. In 2007, the State Council promulgated the Regulations on Employment of Disabled Persons. In 2008, the Standing Committee of the NPC revised Law on Protection of Disabled Persons of People's Republic of China. All government actions reflect the intention of promoting the employment for the disabled and protecting their legal rights relating to work. By the end of 2007, the number for employment of disabled persons reached 4.34 million in urban areas and 16.97 million in rural areas according to the Ministry of Labour and Social Security.

59. See *The Laws of the People's Republic of China 1990–1992* (Science Press, Beijing 1993), at p. 123.

Chapter 8. Covenants of Non-competition; Inventions by Employees

§1. Covenants of Non-competition

231. There is increasing concern in Chinese labour law regarding how to prevent an employee, at the end of his labour contract, from taking a job with a competitor of his previous employer or from setting up in a competing business. The Labour Contract Law states generally that the personnel subject to non-competition are limited to the employer's senior management, senior technicians and other personnel with a confidentiality obligation. The scope, territory and term of the non-competition shall be agreed upon by the employer and the employee, and such agreement shall not violate laws and regulations. It seems that an employer is to decide on whether imposing the non-competition obligations on those employees who have access to the confidential information. With respect to an employee's confidentiality obligation under the labour contract, see Chapter 2.

232. Since the middle of the 1980s, scientists, technicians and other professionals have been permitted in principle to engage in outside scientific work in their spare time for commercial purposes, on the condition that such work does not violate the technological rights and interests of their own employing units with prior approval by the employer. The income thereby derived shall be distributed between the scientists and their own employing units, and is subject to income tax. The practice follows the 1988 State Science Commission's Opinion on Several Issues regarding Scientists and Technicians Who Hold Positions Concurrently.[60] Article 2 thereof forbids such part-time outside work to those (i) who are involved with state secrets; (ii) who are working on state projects; (iii) who hold an important position in their own employing units; and (iv) who have any conflict of interests with the units for which they work on a part-time basis. It is not until the promulgation of the Labour Contract Law of 2007 which requires that the employer shall pay economic compensation to the worker on a monthly basis during the term of the non-competition after the rescission or termination of the labour contract; or if the worker breaches the non-competition provisions, he/she shall pay penalties to the employer as specified. Noticeably, the term of non-competition restriction is not allowed for more than two years after the rescission or termination of the labour contract. Nevertheless, according to Article 9 of the Interpretation of the Supreme Court on Several Issues Concerning the Application of Law in the Trial of Labour Contract Cases (IV) (Judicial Interpretation), if the employer asks to terminate the agreement during the non-competition period, the court shall uphold the claim by the employer who shall, however, pay the employee non-competition compensation for three months. When the employee in breach of the non-competition agreement, after paying the penalty, the employee should resume his non-competition obligation when the employer requests so (Article 10 of the Judicial Interpretation (IV)).

60. See *Complete Book of China's Labour Law* (Xinhua 1994), at p. 196.

§2. Inventions by Employees

233. Both the Chinese Constitution and the Labour Act advocate workers carrying out scientific research, technical innovation, invention and creation. Legal protection for the invention by employees is provided for in the 1984 Patent Law of the PRC (as amended in 1992, 2000 and 2008).[61] The invention by employees is specifically categorized by the Patent Law as a service invention-creation. Article 11 of the 2001 Implementing Regulations of the Patent Law of the PRC[62] defines 'service-invention' to include any invention-creation:

(i) in the course of performing his own duty;
(ii) in execution of any task, other than his own duty, which was entrusted to him by the entity to which he belongs; and
(iii) within one year from his resignation, retirement or change of work, where the invention-creation relates to his own duty or the other task entrusted to him by the entity to which he previously belonged.
In addition to the above definition, the draft Service Invention Regulations (2015) proposed that a service invention should include an invention which is completed mainly by using resources of the employer (e.g. funds, equipment, spare parts, raw materials, reproductive materials or technical information not disclosed to public). Unless an agreement between employers and employees regarding the royalties and return of the funds is in place, then such inventions would not be regarded as service invention (Article 7).

234. Article 6 of the Patent Law provides that for a service invention-creation, made by a person in execution of the tasks of the entity to which he belongs or made by him mainly by using the material and technical means of the entity, the right to apply for a patent belongs to the entity. After the application is approved, the entity shall be the patentee. For any non-service invention-creation, the right to apply for a patent belongs to the inventor or creator. After the application is approved, the inventor or creator shall be the patentee. Article 16 of the Patent Law states that the inventor or creator of a service invention-creation shall be rewarded by the entity being granted such a patent right. In addition, the inventor or creator shall be paid a reasonable remuneration upon exploitation of the patented invention-creation subject to the range of application of such patented invention-creation and the economic benefits it yields.

61. See Patent Law, *Trade Mark Law and Copyright Law of the People's Republic of China* (Law Press China 2002), at p. 2.
62. See China Laws for Foreign Business Regulation CCH International 11-603.

Chapter 9. Settlement of Labour Disputes

§1. Parties to Labour Disputes and the Content of Labour Disputes

235. Settlement of labour disputes stands for handling matters in dispute between subjects governed by the law and regulations. It is noted that the subjects (parties) in labour disputes are referred to as enterprises and workers in the 1993 Regulations on the Settlement of Labour Dispute in Enterprises (which was nullified in 2011). Labour disputes between state agencies, institutions, social organizations and their workers and between private businesses and their assistants and apprentices may be handled by reference to these regulations according to Article 39 of the Regulations on the Settlement of Labour Dispute in Enterprises. However, the Labour Act governs not only labour relations between enterprises and their workers, but also between employing units including individual economic organizations, state agencies, institutions and social organizations and workers with whom a contractual labour relationship is established. The existence of a contractual labour relationship is an essential element for the determination of the type of parties involved in disputes who will be subject to Regulations on the Settlement of Labour Dispute in Enterprises and the Labour Act. In 1997, Chinese authority in charge of personnel employed in administration agencies and public institutions promulgated a separate rules governing certain labour related disputes between such agencies or institutions and their employed personnel. In 2007, the Standing Committee of the NPC promulgate the Law of People's Republic of China on Mediation and Arbitration of Labour Disputes, which became effect on 1 May 2008. Rules on the Handling of Arbitration Cases Involving Labour and Employment Disputes (2009) governed the labour disputes between state agencies and social institutions with their employees. These Rules were replaced by the 2017 version.

236. Interpretation of the Supreme Court on Several Issues Concerning the Application of Law in the Trial of Labour Contract Cases (I), (II), (III) and (IV) were promulgated in 2001, 2006, 2010 and 2013 respectively. The Law on Mediation and Arbitration of Labour Disputes of 2007 applies to the settlement of labour disputes between employing units and labourers within the territory of the PRC. According to the Law, the following labour relationship shall be subject to this Law: (i) disputes arising from the confirmation of labour relations; (ii) disputes arising from the conclusion, performance, alteration and termination of labour contracts; (iii) disputes arising from name removal, dismissal, resignation; (iv) disputes arising from working hours, rest days and leave days, social insurance welfare benefits, training and labour protection; (v) disputes arising from labour remuneration, medical expenses for injury at work, economic compensation or damages; or (vi) other labour disputes prescribed by laws and regulations. Collective labour disputes will be discussed separately in Part II.

237. Labour contractual disputes are described as disputes arising from the performance of the labour contract.[63] Disputes arising from the performance of the labour contract were interpreted by the former Ministry of Labour as being disputes in implementation, modification, revocation and termination of the labour contract.[64] The Interpretation of the Supreme Court on Several Issues Concerning the Application of Law in the Trial of Labour Contract Cases (I) added disputes arising from establishing labour relations without a labour contract, disputes caused by retired employees' claim for social insurance, disputes of employees' claim (i) for getting back a deposit, mortgage payment or property, transfer of personnel file and social insurance upon termination of the labour contract; (ii) for job-related injury; (iii) due to restructuring of the employing unit; and (iv) economic compensation for remuneration, overtime, and minimum salary according to Article 85 of the Labour Contract Law.

238. In accordance with the Interpretation of the Supreme Court on Several Issues Concerning the Application of Law in the Trial of Labour Contract Cases (II), the following are not considered as labour disputes:

(i) disputes between employees and social insurance organization on social insurance issues;
(ii) disputes between employees and employing units due to the transfer of state-owned housing resulting from housing reform;
(iii) disputes of employees over the identification of disability degree or occupational diseases by the professional authority;
(iv) disputes between a family and persons performing housekeeping services;
(v) disputes between individual craftsman and helpers, apprentices;
(vi) disputes between rural contractors and their employees.

§2. MEDIATION AND ARBITRATION

239. With the implementation of the 1993 Regulations on the Settlement of Labour Disputes in Enterprises (invalid since 2011) and the 1994 Labour Act, the labour dispute process involved mediation and arbitration. Voluntary consultations between the parties themselves, mediation and arbitration are alternative means of resolving labour disputes outside the courts. Article 79 of the Labour Act states that labour disputes may be settled either through mediation by an enterprise's labour dispute mediation committee or through arbitration by a labour arbitration committee of the labour administration. Mediation is not a required procedure for entering arbitration, rather merely one form of settling labour disputes.

---

63. See Article 2 of the Regulations on the Settlement of Labour Dispute in Enterprise, 1993.
64. See Interpretation concerning Several Issues in the Regulations on the Settlement of Labour Dispute in Enterprises of the PRC, 1993 in *Complete Book of China's Labour Law* (Xinhua 1994), at p. 1217.

240. It is up to the parties to choose directly to settle disputes either through arbitration or mediation. If the parties choose to resolve their labour disputes by mediation with their enterprise's labour disputes mediation committee, the committee shall conclude the mediation within 15 days after the application for mediation has been accepted by the committee. If the mediation fails to reach agreement, or if one party does not implement the mediation agreement, the parties or the other party may apply to an arbitration committee for arbitration.

241. In accordance with Law of the People's Republic of China on Mediation and Arbitration of Labour Disputes (promulgated in 2007 and taking effect in 2008), labour dispute committees include: labour-dispute mediation commissions of enterprises; people's mediation institutions at the grass-roots level established in accordance with law; organizations with the function of labour-dispute mediation established in townships or neighbourhoods. In accordance with Provisions on Negotiation and Mediation of Labour Disputes of Enterprises (promulgated in 2011) the enterprise mediation committee consists of representatives for the workers and the enterprise with equal number. The employee representatives shall be the members of the labour union committee or nominated and elected by all the employees of the enterprise, the enterprise's representatives shall be designated by the person-in-charge of the enterprise. The chairman of the mediation committee shall be a member of the labour union committee or a person nominated by both parties.

242. In mediating labour disputes, the mediation committee shall follow the principle of voluntary participation of the two parties. If an agreement is reached upon mediation, a written mediation agreement shall be signed by the two parties and the chairman of the mediation committee (or mediator) and stamped by the mediation committee. The mediation agreement shall be implemented by the parties. If the mediation has failed, a written mediation opinion shall record the situation and be signed by the chairman of the mediation committee and stamped by the mediation committee. If no mediation agreement is reached within 15 days upon the receipt of the mediation application, either party may submit the dispute for arbitration. Noticeably, a mediation agreement on matters relating to monetary or compensatory payment is enforceable by the court directly in accordance with the Law on Mediation and Arbitration of Labour Disputes of 2007.

243. The labour arbitration committee under the labour administration is set up at county level. In accordance with Article 81 of the Labour Act, the labour arbitration committee is composed of representatives of the labour administration department, a trade union at the same level and employing units. There should be an odd number of personnel on the labour arbitration committee. It is chaired by the chief arbitrator. However, for simple arbitration case, one arbitrator may try the case. Noticeably, the arbitration process is for free of charge since the implementing of the Labour Contract Law and Law on Mediation and Arbitration of Labour Disputes in 2008. The local government shall finance the arbitration body and its daily operation.

244. The labour arbitration committee implements a system of arbitrators and arbitration tribunals for handling labour disputes. The labour arbitration committee shall be composed of personnel of the labour administration or of other relevant government departments, trade unionists and of the enterprise, while the arbitrator must have the qualification of having experience as a judge, or working in the fields of legal or teaching with intermediate professional title, or with at least five years' working experience in human resource management or trade union, or lawyer with at least three years of licensed practice. The arbitration tribunal normally consists of three arbitrators, and simple disputes may be dealt with by one arbitrator.

245. In accordance with Article 82 of the Labour Act, a party to a labour dispute is required to apply in writing to the labour arbitration committee for arbitration within 60 days from the date of the occurrence of the labour dispute. However, the Labour Contract Law the Law on Mediation and Arbitration of Labour Disputes stipulates that the time limit for application for arbitration in labour disputes is one year, calculated from the date when either party to the dispute knew or should have known the infringement of his rights. An extension of the period of time for one year would be in favour of migrant workers from countryside who are mostly paid once a year by the year end. For the same reason, in accordance with the Law on Mediation and Arbitration, a dispute arising from employer's delay in making payment of wages during the employment period is not subject to the time limit for the arbitration. The labour arbitration committee will normally make an arbitration award within 45 days of acceptance of an application for arbitration. Fifteen days for an extension as a maximum may be granted by the head of labour arbitration committee. If no arbitration award is made in due time, parties may institute legal proceedings in a people's court, in accordance with the Law on Mediation and Arbitration of Labour Disputes of 2007.

246. During the process of arbitration, mediation is conducted first. If an agreement can be reached voluntarily through mediation, the labour arbitration tribunal will prepare a mediation statement based on the contents of the agreement. The mediation statement made by the labour arbitration tribunal will be effective as of the date of the signature by the parties confirming receipt of the statement.

247. If no agreement is reached in mediation or a party changes its mind before the mediation statement has been delivered to the recipient, the labour arbitration tribunal shall make an arbitration award on time. The arbitration award can either confirm or overrule an administrative decision made by an employer and provide him with arbitration suggestions regarding that administrative decision. To those disputes involved in economic compensation, the arbitration award may modify a previous administrative measure imposed on an employee based on the enterprise's internal rule. The arbitration award shall have legal binding force, if the case is not brought before the court within 15 days.[65] When one party neither files a suit within the lawful period nor complies with the arbitration award, the other party may apply

65. Article 30 of the Regulations on Settlement of Labour Dispute in Enterprises and Article 50 of the Law on Mediation and Arbitration of Labour Disputes.

to the people's court for enforcement of the award.[66] Importantly, except for very limited and restrictive statutory grounds, an employer may not challenge, through judicial means, such arbitration award being final and legally effective on disputes over monetary pay for the amount no more than 12 months' minimum wage amount at the locale and such arbitrations award on disputes over implementing of state labour standards concerning working time, rest and social security. The arbitration award on the disputed matters not as being mentioned above may be denied by either party who summits the disputing case to the court within 15 days upon the receipt of the arbitration award.

248. However, the enforcement of an arbitral award or mediation statement will be subject to examination and verification by the courts. In accordance with Article 213 of the 1991 Civil Procedural Law of the PRC (revised in 2007), the court may refuse recognition of an arbitration award on the ground, *inter alia*, that the matter of arbitration exceeds the scope of the jurisdiction of the arbitration tribunal, the composition of the arbitration tribunal or the arbitrate proceedings violate the legal procedure, or because of insufficient evidence and incorrect application of the law. If the court notifies to the parties its decision not to enforce an arbitration award or an effective mediation statement, the court shall also notify the parties that the labour dispute may be brought before the court for court trial.

§3. Court Proceeding

249. Labour dispute litigation is the ultimate judicial relief of the parties to a labour dispute. A labour dispute case can be submitted to court for litigation only after complying with the mandatory labour arbitration process. The Law of PRC on Mediation and Arbitration of Labour Disputes regulates that labour dispute cases may be submitted to courts if the case has been rejected by the labour arbitration committee, if one of the parties appeals to revoke or not enforce a final arbitral award, or if the parties are not satisfied with the arbitral award. In addition, the Interpretation of the Supreme Court on Several Issues Concerning the Application of Law in the Trial of Labour Contract Cases (I-IV) also defines special practical cases which could be brought to the courts.

250. In filing a court case, the court will examine whether the parties in dispute have contractual labour relations governed by the Labour Act or any other applicable regulation. Staff in state agencies, institutions and social organizations in which no labour contractual relationship has been established will not come under the scope of the application of the Labour Act. The qualified parties to the labour disputes shall also follow the time limit for the court to take the labour dispute case.

66. Article 83 of Labour Act and Article 31 of the Regulations on Settlement of Labour Dispute in Enterprises.

Labour dispute litigation cases are handled under the jurisdiction of basic-level people's court in general in the location of the employer or place where the labour contract is performed.

251. In principle, the burden of proof rests on the plaintiff in the labour dispute trial. In order to avoid possible unfairness due to positioning of the parties in the labour relationship, Interpretation of the Supreme People's Court on Several Issues Concerning the Application of Law in the Trial of Labour Contract Cases (I) makes it clear that the employers shall assume the burden of proof if the disputes arise from unilateral termination of labour contract by the employer, reduction of labour remuneration, calculation of years of services etc. Interpretation of the Supreme Court on Several Issues Concerning the Application of Law in the Trial of Labour Contract Cases (III) permits exception for the above rule of evidence. The employee shall bear the burden of proof for his claim for overtime payment. However, the burden of proof will be shifted to the employer in this regard if the employee proves that the employer refuses to provide the proof in its hand.

252. Since 1986, The Civil Procedural Law of the PRC (on Trial Bases), replaced by the 1991 Civil Procedural Law of the PRC (as revised in 2007, 2012 and 2017), has applied the procedure of handling labour dispute cases by the people's court. In general, under the Civil Procedural Law of the PRC, when instituting an action, two conditions shall be met, namely, the plaintiff shall be an individual, legal person or other organization with a direct interest in the case; there shall be a specific defendant.

253. In addition, a labour dispute case can be brought before the court only on the condition that the matter has been dealt with by the labour arbitration tribunal and when the parties (or one party) to the labour dispute disagree(s) with the arbitration award, he may then file a suit at the people's court within 15 days of being notified of it.[67] If no arbitration award is made after a time limit or a non-acceptance for arbitration is notified by the labour arbitration tribunal, a party in disagreement may not initiate administrative litigation against the labour arbitration tribunal. The court may, however, accept the labour dispute case for a trial subject to the Supreme People's Court's Interpretation on Several Issues in Application of the Laws in Handling Labour Disputes (I).

254. The principle of mediation also applies to judicial proceedings. A court decision will be made after the trial which follows the procedure for trying a civil case. The decision may overrule the administrative measurements made by an employer based on the enterprise's internal rule. It is unclear in the existing legislation whether the court decision can modify the administrative measures imposed on an employee based on the enterprise's internal rule.

67. Article 83 of the Labour Act.

Part II. Collective Labour Relations

Chapter 1. Trade Union Freedom

§1. Ideology and Concept

255. The 'glorious working class' was regarded as the governing class of the state[68] in socialist countries. Workers were not subject to contractual employment relationships, previously seen as a mode of exploitation of employees, as sellers of their own labour to a capitalist employer.[69] The presumption had been that because ownership of the means of production was held by the working class and labourers, who in turn exercise state power, the interest of the state and the workers should be fundamentally the same or at least coincide. This theory implies, with regard to collective labour relations, that trade unions should not be organized as a mechanism for confronting the state or employers. The Union movement must be in the interests of the whole working class.

256. Trade unions are the 'conveyor belts' of the Communist Party which is deemed to be the leading force of the proletariat. The concept is that the Communist Party transmits its policy and directives to the organized labourers to gain their direct support and guide the union's movement in the context of proletariat revolution. It is not possible to have a trade union independent from the leadership of the Communist Party to represent and protect workers' immediate interests only.

257. Related to such an idea is the workers' right to organize and to strike, which had been the revolutionary weapon against the bourgeoisie government and eventually would overthrow it. Workers in socialist China would not and should not use the right to strike against their own proletariat government, hence there is no constitutional basis for the right to strike.[70] The Labour Act is silent on this issue. In practice, collective strike action is even considered to be ultimately detrimental to the workers themselves. In recent years, the form of the collective action was seen as taking a walk collectively. There are various NGOs which claim to act on behalf of migrant workers and workers of other informal sectors. Such NGOs often meet

68. See Preamble and Article 1 of The Constitution of the People's Republic of China (1982).
69. See K. Marx, *Capital*, pp. 270–280 (B. Fowkes ed. 1977).
70. The right to strike was not stipulated by the 1954 Constitution, but was added to the 1975 and 1978 Constitutions. It was eliminated in the 1982 Constitution.

legal difficulty in being officially registered (see paragraph 292) and they are sometimes busy fighting against each other and lack smooth cooperation and coordination.

258. Nonetheless, with the diversity of economic development and the adoption of the so-called socialist commodity theories in the 1980s which was later further revised as the socialist market economy in the 1990s, differences of interests between individuals, collectives and state have been more and more recognized. Generally speaking, in the pre-reform era, unions were primarily concerned with promoting production and strive to implementing the state plan, whereas in the reform period, unions are more engaged in conciliating conflict between various parties due to the differences of interests. With the rapid changes of economic and labour policy, the unions have encountered the difficulty of the balance requirement to represent both interests of the Communist Party-State and workers. The idea of trade union autonomy and independence of the unions has been more or less concerned with workers and authority. However, the legal restriction upon the right to establish an independent trade union and the right to choose one's own union still remains, since there is only one officially recognized union organization.

§2. Freedom to Establish and Join Unions

259. The freedom of assembly and association provided for in Article 35 of the Constitution does not establish the concept for pluralism in the trade union organization. The 1992 Trade Union Law (as amended in 2001 and 2009) stipulates that the All-China Federation of Trade Union (ACFTU) shall be established as the unified national organization (Art. 10). In other words, no separate unions are protected by law. All unions in the territory of the PRC are subject to this unified organizational structure. At the apex, is the ACFTU that leads the national industrial trade union, local trade union federation and local industrial trade union. At the bottom, a basic-level trade union committee may be set up in an enterprise, an institution or a state organ with a membership of 25 or more.

260. Neither the Labour Act nor the Trade Union Law explicitly state whether there is freedom to join or not to join a union of one's own choice and to withdraw from a union, though Article 2 of the Trade Union specifies that trade unions are mass organizations of the working class formed by the workers and staff members on a voluntary basis. It is noted that the voluntary basis to form the trade union organization refers only to the one particular trade union. Therefore, there is no possible choice of joining this or another union.

261. In addition, under Article 11 of the Trade Union Law, approval of the establishment of a trade union is required to be obtained from a higher level trade union organization in a hierarchical structure as described above. Against these legal limits, Article 3 of the Trade Union Law proclaimed that all manual or mental workers who rely on wages or salaries as their main source of income, irrespective of their nationality, race, sex, occupation, religion or educational background, have the right to organize and join trade unions according to the law. Along the same line, Article 7 of the Labour Act also provides that the right to join and organize a union is required to be subject to the law.

262. Under Article 4 of the Trade Union Law, the trade unions shall observe and safeguard the Constitution (including the 'Four Cardinal Principles', see paragraph 9), take it as the fundamental criteria for their activities and conduct their work in an independent and autonomous way in accordance with the Constitution of the ACFTU. In line with the above prescribed stipulations in the Trade Union Law, Article 18 of the Company Law also stresses that the employees of a company shall, according to the law, organize a trade union and conduct union activities.

263. It is not hard to understand why China has ratified neither the Freedom of Association and Protection of the Right to Organize Convention 1948 (No. 87), nor the Right to Organize and Collective Bargaining Convention, 1949 (No. 98), though the ILO's Committee on Freedom of Association urged the Chinese government 'to ensure that the right of workers to establish organizations of their own choosing and the right of these organizations to function freely are recognized in the country's legislation and practice'.[71]

§3. Rights and Duties of Trade Unions

I. Rights of Trade Unions

264. China's trade union law adopts Lenin's teaching about a trade union's 'dual safeguarding function', namely its function to safeguard the overall interests of state and society as well as its function to safeguard the concrete interests of workers. Article 6 of the Trade Union Law stipulates that while protecting the overall interests of the entire Chinese people, trade unions shall safeguard the legitimate rights and interests of the workers and staff members. This provision sets out a collectivism, rather than a syndicalism footing with respect to the rights and duties of the trade unions in Chinese labour law. Trade unions have certain right to access to information relating to the interests of the employees, to solicit opinions from employees, to request and recommend a proper way to deal with the matters relating to the interests of the employees.

265. With respect to trade unions' right in safeguarding the concrete rights and interests of employees, the Trade Union Law itself does not provide detailed procedures for unions' bargaining position in payment, conditions of work or grievance handling and other employment matters. The law states simply that unions have the right to request an employer to rectify himself if the employer violates labour law; to help the employee to sign the labour contract with the employer and they may on behalf of the employees sign collective agreements with an employer

71. See 279th Report of the Committee on Freedom of Association regarding case No. 1500; see also 275th, 281st and 286th Reports of the Committee on Freedom of Association (Geneva, ILO).

(Art. 20); to advance their opinion on unfair dismissal (Art. 21); to participate mediation and arbitration of labour disputes and render their support to an employee in the settlement of disputes (Arts. 21 and 28); to submit suggestions on working conditions as well as on safety and public health facilities (Art. 23); to suggest solutions when the management has compelled workers to carry out dangerous work (Art. 24); to investigate violation cases (Art. 25).

266. With respect to the participation of democratic management, according to Article 19 of the Trade Union Law, the trade unions have the right to safeguard the democratic management system carried out basically through the workers congress. As the working organization of the workers' congress, the trade union committee at enterprise level has the right to advance its opinions if the enterprise acts in contravention to the system of the workers' congress or other system of democratic management. In a state enterprise, as the trade union committee is in charge of the day-to-day work of the workers congress, it organizes for workers to participate in democratic management through the workers congress and supervises the implementation of its decisions made within the power prescribed to it by the Law of the PRC on Industrial Enterprises Owned by the Whole People. Article 38 and 39 of the Trade Union Law requires that the trade union shall be represented in the management committee of the enterprise[72] and in addition, any meeting held by the enterprises discussing matters on wages, welfare, safety in production, labour protection and labour insurance and other issues related to the vital interests of the workers shall be attended by a trade union representative(s).

267. In a collectively owned enterprise, the workers congress has more direct and democratic power, and the trade union committee in collectively owned enterprises is called on by the Trade Union Law to fully support and organize participation of the workers in democratic management, supervise and defend their right to elect and remove managerial personnel and to decide on major issues concerning operation and management.[73]

268. Enterprises with foreign investment are required to listen to the opinions of the trade unions, while making studies and decisions on issues of wages, welfare, safety in production, labour protection and labour insurance which affect the vital interests of the workers. The Implementing Regulations of the Law of the PRC on Sino-Foreign Equity Joint Ventures gives union representatives the right to attend the meetings of the board of directors of joint ventures on issues such as development plans, production and operational activities. Though union representatives have no right of vote at such board meetings, they may submit opinions and requests of workers. In deciding labour-related matters, the board of directors of joint ventures is required to heed the opinions of the labour union and win its co-operation.

---

72. The committee is a body to assist director of an enterprise in making decision on the important issues of management – Article 47 of the Law of the PRC on Industrial Enterprises Owned by the Whole People provides the mandatory bases for the establishment of such committee. However, the provisions of the Law are largely superseded in fact by legislation concerning corporation.
73. See Article 36 of the Trade Union Law.

269. New developments in corporation law require companies to listen to the opinions of their trade unions and employees when studying and deciding specified labour issues, issues concerning major production and operations as well as when the companies formulate important rules and regulations.[74] A representative of the unions or employees shall be invited to be the member of the governing body of a company.[75]

270. Trade unions have the right to exercise democratic supervision of their enterprises and government. The Trade Union Law provides a basis for such supervision rights to enterprises, especially the right to state their opinions regarding enterprises' violation of the system of the workers' congress or other systems of democratic management and the right to investigate violation of the legal rights and interests of the workers by enterprises, institutions and government agencies. However, the scope and procedures for exercise of such right to investigate, especially the limit to investigate government agencies in exercising their administrative authorities *ultra vires* is not clearly regulated in existing labour law.

271. According to Article 28 of the Trade Union Law, the supervision right is also exercised in relation to the trade union's participation in an enterprise's mediation of labour disputes and its participation in local labour arbitration organization.

272. Another matter subject to trade union supervision laid down in Article 23 of the Trade Union Law is that trade unions may advance their opinions on working conditions and labour safety and public health facilities in newly built or extended enterprises and in technological transformation projects. Chinese law and practice in occupational safety and health require that the safety and public health facilities be designed, constructed and put into operation simultaneously with the development of projects in the building of new enterprises, in the expansion of the enterprises or in technological transformation. Such project test and acceptance verification with respect to design, construction and operation of the safety and public health facilities must be conducted with the participation of trade unions, labour authorities, public health authorities and environment protection authorities.

273. In carrying out their supervision right over the government, in accordance with Article 33 of the Trade Union Law, the trade unions have the right to submit their opinions regarding local development planning and local legislation relating to the rights and interests of employees. In addition, local governments at and above

74. See Articles 18 of the Company Law (latest revised in 2013).
75. See Article 108 of the Company Law (latest revised in 2013). The members of the board of directors of a limited liability company invested in and established by two or more state-owned enterprises, or by two or more other state-owned investment entities shall include representatives of the staff and workers of that company (Art. 44 of the Company Law). In addition, Articles 51 and 117 of the Company Law require that a supervisory board, in a limited liability company with a relatively large scale operation and in a company limited by shares, shall be established, and be composed of representatives of shareholders and an appropriate proportion of representatives of the company's staff and workers.

county level are obliged to consult the trade unions in formulating important policies or taking any measures in respect of wages, prices, safety in production, as well as labour protection and labour insurance. Article 34 of the Trade Union Law further calls upon local governments and trade unions to set up appropriate communication channels through which the government would inform trade unions about the important work plans of the government and about administrative arrangements related to the trade unions' work. Importantly, such channels are expected to enable both the government and the trade unions to study and deal with issues submitted by the employees and by the masses. Generally, in dealing with the relationship of the government and the trade unions, a cooperative approach is adopted by Chinese labour law.

II. Duties of Trade Unions

274. Trade unions undertake to mobilize and educate workers in order to 'turn them into well-educated and self-disciplined labourers with lofty ideals and moral integrity', as described by Article 7 of the Trade Union Law. The content of such education includes education in patriotism, collectivism, socialism, democracy and the legal system, labour discipline, and science, culture and technology. The trade unions' efforts to mobilize and educate workers are part of the mission of the unions to reinforce the country's political and economic system.

275. The trade unions have a duty to support and assist management in exercising its functions and powers, especially in the case of a work-stoppage or slowdown. It is notable that Article 27 of the Trade Union Law urges the trade unions to conciliate disputes in the event of a work stoppage or slowdown and to consult with the management, in order to meet the reasonable demands of workers so as to restore normal production as soon as possible. Although such a provision is compromise oriented, and the Chinese word for 'strike' is avoided, this is the only reference in the national labour legislation which touches upon the existence of strike action, and the implication is that the right to strike is not banned, while it is not enshrined in the existing Constitution. Certainly, it is not anticipated under this provision that the right to strike is to be granted to workers and the right to organize strike action is to be permitted to the trade unions. It merely puts the trade unions in the position of being obliged to deal with spontaneous stoppages or go-slow actions.

276. Articles 30 and 31 of the Trade Union Law recognize the trade unions' usual functions in providing collective welfare, organizing entertainment for employees in their spare time, organizing recreational and sports activities, and organizing cultural and technical studies and vocational training.

Chapter 2. The Trade Unions and Employers' Associations

§1. Organizational Structure

277. The trade union organization had been established after the founding of the People's Republic of China under the Trade Union Law of the PRC (adopted by the Committee of the People's Central Government on 28 June 1950) with latest revision in 2009. In the late 1950s and 1960s the role of the All-China Federation of Trade Unions (ACFTU) was reduced due to dramatic political changes, and was eventually replaced by the All-China Red Worker Rebel General Corps during the Great Cultural Revolution. The All-China Federation of Trade Unions was rehabilitated in 1978, and in October 1978, the trade unions held their Ninth National Congress. Since then the National Congress of the ACFTU has been held every five years and the latest been the 16th National Congress in 2013. At that Congress, the Trade Union Constitution was revised to add the guideline of leadership of the Communist Party of China and the guidance of Marxism-Leninism, Mao Zedong ideologies, Deng Xiaoping's theory, the 'Three Represents' (the Communist Part of China represents Chinese advanced productive forces, the orientation of Chinese advanced culture and benefits of people) and scientific outlook on development.

278. Article 9 of the Trade Union Law provides that the organizational principle of the trade unions is the principle of democratic centralism. The application of this principle is that (i) trade union committees at various levels must be democratically elected by the union members' congresses or union members' representative congress; (ii) trade union committees at various levels are responsible for and report to the union members' congresses or union member representatives' congresses at the corresponding level and subject to their supervision as well; (iii) the union members' congresses or union member representatives congresses have the right to recall or remove an elected member of the trade union committees; (iv) the lower level trade union organizations are subject to the leadership of the higher level of the trade unions.

279. The trade union committees (including the executive committee of the ACFTU, trade unions committee of the trade union federation at various local level and basic-level trade union committees) exercise executive and leading functions when the national union member representative congress and local representative assemblies are not in session. The executive committee of the ACFTU and trade union committee of the trade union federation at various local levels are elected by the national union member representative congress and various local representative assemblies respectively. Basic-level trade union committees are elected by the trade union member assembly or trade union representative assembly. According to Article 9 of the Trade Union Law, trade union committees are responsible, and report their work to the representative congress at their respective levels and are subject to their supervision as well. However, the national union member representative congress is held once every five years and local representative assemblies are held once every three years. Noticeably, enterprises must not transfer or mobilize the job of the full-time chairman and vice-chairman of the trade union when they are during the term of office. If a job transfer is really necessary, the consent of the trade union committee as well as the higher-level committee must be obtained (Art. 17). In addition, the Chairman, Vice Chairman and member of the trade union committee shall have their labour contracts extended until the end of their office term (Art. 18).

280. The Trade Union Law imposes a single trade union structure. The unified national trade union organization is the All-China Federation of Trade Unions (ACFTU). The trade union federations are established at and above the county level. Industrial trade unions may be formed at national or local levels for single industries or several industries of a similar nature. A basic-level trade union committee may be set up in an enterprise, an institution or a state organ.

The ACFTU leads the national industrial trade unions, local trade union federation and local industrial trade union. Local industrial trade unions are led by local trade union federation as well as by the national organizations of industrial trade union. The establishment of the organization of the national industrial trade union is determined by the ACFTU.

281. Basic-level trade union committees are led by the trade union federation at county level. Those basic-level trade union committees which also belong to certain industrial trade union organizations are subject to the leadership of the local trade union federation and of the local industrial trade union as well. The trade union federation at county level and the industrial trade union at provincial level are led by the trade union federations at provincial level. Trade union federations at provincial level and various national organizations of industrial trade unions are led by the ACFTU.

282. To strengthen the control of organization of the trade union at local level, the change has been made that workplaces with more than 25 people can now form unions, whereas previously this was only possible for workplaces with more than 200 people. Unionizing large numbers of workers in the private sector, service establishments and enterprises with foreign investment has been considered. The Vice Chairman of ACFTU stated in 2012 at the 3rd Presidium Meeting of the 15th National Congress that 82 per cent of workers in private enterprises had established trade unions.

283. The official national employers' organization is the China Enterprises Directors' Association (CEDA). Local employers' organizations at provincial level are established to represent local interests of the employers. In the state planned economy with the domination of the state ownership, the right of employers to organize has not been provided, because directors and managers were state enterprises cadres representing state interests. Provisions regarding employers' organizations are still in development. In recent years, private entrepreneurs in some localities have organized their own organizations such as 'Chambers of Private Enterprises', 'Guilds of non-governmental Enterprises' and 'Foreign-invested Enterprises Associations'. The Labour Act, however, is silent about the independence of employers' organizations and the pluralism of the employers' organizational structure. CEDA consists of entrepreneur (employer) and entrepreneur group, is registered with the Ministry of Civil Affairs of the PRC and is a non-profit legal person. CEDA provides service to entrepreneurs (employers), following the principle of abiding by the Constitution, laws, regulations, national policies and the social morals; safeguarding the legitimate rights and interests of entrepreneurs (employers); promoting the law-abiding and self-discipline of entrepreneurs (employers); playing the role of bridge between entrepreneurs (employers) and government, and coordinating the relationship between managers and labourers. It has the official role of participating in the work of the tripartite consultation mechanism for coordinating labour relations and as a member of the Tripartite representative on behalf of the Chinese employers ' organization.

§2. Role of the Trade Unions and Employers' Associations

284. In order to ensure that workers conform to the central Communist Party politically and ideologically, the trade unions have been called upon to carry out the party's decisions and maintain workers' political correctness. The Trade Union Law makes it clear that the law enables unions to serve socialist modernization. It is acknowledged that unions are the means to be used to strengthen the existing structure of the socialist system.

285. Unions play a role in mobilizing workers to strive to fulfil production targets by educating workers to approach their work with the right attitude and to observe labour discipline (Art. 7 of the Trade Union Law).

286. Unions are also to play their role in representing and protecting workers' interests on behalf of employees by presenting their opinion to the government in policy making and planning, participating in collective consultations and in dispute resolution etc. The trade unions' role in their relations to the state and workers is consistent with their 'dual safeguarding function' as described in paragraph 266 above. For the discussion of trade unions' dual role (see also Introduction, §4, II).

287. Employers' organizations at provincial and national level have stipulated roles in fixing minimum wages as discussed in Part I, Chapter 4, §2. However, in the context of the collective consultation, employers' organizations do not seem to play any significant role, since the collective agreement is now only drawn up at enterprise level. Only when the collective bargaining process is adopted at industrial or national level, may employers' organizations at a corresponding level play their role to represent the interests of the employers concerned. Nevertheless, employers' organizations are generally seen as pro-reform forces in China's enterprise reform. Employers' organizations provide some kind of forum for employers to represent the position of management and to promote autonomy of the enterprises.

§3. Legal Status of Trade Unions and Employers' Associations

288. In order to legally protect the organization of the trade union. Article 14 of the Trade Union Law explicitly clarifies that the ACFTU, a local trade union federation or an industrial trade union enjoys legal person status of a social association, one of the forms of non-profit legal person under 2017 General Rules of the Civil Law of the People's Republic of China. Chinese civil law differentiates between profit legal persons, non-profit legal persons (such as institutions, social associations, foundations, and social service agencies) and special legal persons.[76] Trade union organizations and employers' associations belong to the category of the social organizations which may acquire the legal person status if they meet the requirements for a legal person in the capacity of a social association.

289. A legal person is defined by Article 36 of the General Principles of the Civil Law and Article 57 of the General Rules of the Civil Law as an organization with the capacity of the civil right and the capacity of the civil act and, according to the law, independently enjoys civil rights and assumes civil obligation. With a legal person status, the trade union's capacity of the civil right and the capacity of the civil act commence when it is formed and cease when it is dissolved. The ACFTU, a local trade union federation or an industrial trade union will be qualified as a legal person from the time of its establishment and will act independently in civil relation with its capacity of the civil right and the capacity of the civil act. However, basic-level trade union committees will not necessarily acquire legal person status when they are established, unless they satisfy the legal requirements and acquire legal personality according to the law.[77]

290. According to Article 37 of the General Principles of the Civil Law, the defining characteristics of a legal person are that (i) it is lawfully established (ii) it possesses the necessary property or funds (iii) it has its own name, organizational structure and residence; and (iv) it can assume civil liability independently. Article 50 of the General Principles of the Civil Law states that social organizations which fulfil the requirements for legal person status may acquire such status upon approval or registration, if the law requires registration. Otherwise such organizations shall acquire the legal person status when they are established. Subject to the existing applicable provisions, approval and registration are required for establishment of the social association with the legal person status. The same provisions are repeated in Article 58 of the General Rules of the Civil Law. The establishment of legal persons shall be subject to approval of relevant authorities if laws and administrative regulations so require. Therefore, it is legally difficult for an NGO functioning as an alternative grassroots labourers' organization to be registered under the Trade Union Law and the 1989 Regulation on the Social Organization Registration (amended in 2016).

76. See sections 2 and 3 and 4 of Chapter III of the General Rules of the Civil Law of the PRC.
77. See para. 2 of Article 14 of the Trade Union Law.

291. The China Enterprise Directors' Federation (CEDA) or China Enterprises Association (CEA) had legal person status when it was established. Associations at national level must meet the requirements to be a legal person.

292. The legal person status of the trade union will strengthen the legitimacy of trade union activities, especially with respect to their increasingly representative role in resolving conflict between workers and management. For example, the trade union, on behalf of the workers, acts as a party in its legal capacity to conclude collective agreement with the employer. It may assist an injured employee in a legal suit and get involved with other legal matters to better protect workers' legitimate rights and interests.

293. In accordance with the Trade Union Law, trade unions enjoy guaranteed funding and access to facilities. The sources of the fund are comprised of monthly union membership fees (0.5 per cent of the base salary by individual) and 2 per cent of workers' monthly total wages payroll contributed by the employer (out of which 40 per cent shall be submitted to the high-level trade union), income derived from enterprises and undertakings run by trade unions, state subsidies and other incomes. A trade union will have its own bank account and must manage the fund based on the principle of financial autonomy. Property owned by trade unions is protected by law under Article 77 of the General Principles of the Civil Law. Trade unions also have the right to possess and the right to use or profit from the property which is allocated by the employer or state to trade unions for use and possession. Only the owner of such allocated property has the right to dispose of it. Provisions of Article 46 of the Trade Union Law protect the property owned by the trade union as well as immovable property allocated to trade unions from being occupied, misappropriated or arbitrarily disposed of by any organization or individual.

294. Wages payment and other benefits are guaranteed for trade union activists who give up their working time for the purpose of trade union work, although in principle, basic-level trade union committees must organize their activities after work as required by Article 40 of the Trade Union Law. Under Article 41 of the Trade Union Law, wages and bonuses of full-time trade union functionaries are paid by employers, and their social insurance and other benefit treatment will be the same as that of the normal workers. Thus, economically, full-time union functionaries largely rely on employers' spending or public finance. An employer can easily transfer these functionaries except those who hold trade union chairmen or vice-chairmen positions, as Article 17 of the Trade Union Law requires approval, for such a transfer due to necessity of work, from the trade union committee and its high level trade union. Otherwise a trade union chairman or vice chairman must not be arbitrarily transferred before the expiry of their tenure of office. In some extreme cases, a director or vice-director (general manager or vice-general manager) and the head of the personnel department in an enterprise or a company concurrently hold a position as the trade union chairman. Significantly, retired union functionaries at and above county level will receive the same pension benefit as those of the functionaries of a state organ which are financed by the state budget.[78] This indicates that state backing, from a financial and personnel management point of view, makes it hard to have a clear cut idea of the legal person status of trade unions.

78. See Article 48 of the Trade Union Law.

Chapter 3. Collective Bargaining

§1. INTRODUCTION

295. Collective agreements, cultivated since the early 1980s in Sino-foreign joint ventures, have been further developed by the Labour Act with its accompanying regulations, after more than a decade of labour reform. The mechanism of collective consultation and collective agreement has been added to the contractual protection of labourers' rights. Although the terminology of collective bargaining is not explicitly used either in the 1992 revised Trade Union Law or in the Labour Act, the Trade Union Law recognizes the practice of equal consultations and collective agreements.[79] In Chinese 'collective consultations and discussion' is a more friendly and compromising way of saying 'bargaining' or 'negotiation'. The terminology of collective consultations is also referred to in the 1994 Regulations on Collective Agreements as having the purpose of concluding a collective agreement to conduct consultations and discussions between an enterprise's trade union or employees' representatives and the corresponding enterprise's representatives.[80] In accordance with the Labour Act, the collective consultation was regulated in the Tentative Measures on Collective Negotiation on Salary in 2000. The 2004 Regulations on Collective Agreements (issued by the Ministry of Labour and Social Security, effective as of 1 May 2004) replaced the 1994 Regulations on Collective Agreements. The Labour Contract Law of 2007 enshrined the mechanism of a collective agreement concerning a specific labour-related mater or labour matters in general.

296. A collective agreement is defined by the 2004 Regulations on Collective Agreements as a written agreement to collective consultations between an employer and its employees covering 15 items regarding labour remuneration, working hours, rest and leave, labour health and safety, professional training, insurance, welfare and other matters in accordance with the law and regulations. The similar coverage for provisions of a collective agreement is provided for by the Labour Contract Law. Articles 33, 34 and 35 of the Labour Act describe the content, signing procedures, review and effectiveness of the collective agreement. Article 53 of the Labour Contract Law also puts forward the concepts of industrial or regional collective agreement. However, in reality, the industrial or regional employers' organization plays a limited role in this regard.

297. A model collective agreement was developed by Beijing Jeep Company Ltd, a joint venture between the American General Motor Co. and Beijing Automobile Manufacturer. The agreement was updated in line with Chinese economic reform policy and legal developments during 1984–1993. It brought the Western – or American-style of bargaining process into industrial relations in socialist China and was considered to be a pioneer experiment by the Chinese media.[81] This new

79. See Article 6 of the Trade Union Law.
80. See Article 7 of the Regulations on Collective Agreements which is effective as of 1 January 1995 in China Update: The PRC, *Labour Law* (Asia Law and Practice 1995), at p. 64.
81. See Zhongguo Laodongbao (*China Labour Daily*) 24 February 1994.

practice of collective agreement was promoted by the government, especially in collectively owned enterprises, those enterprises which were restructured into limited liability companies or companies limited by shares and enterprises with foreign investment.[82] Further development of collective bargaining and collective agreement in China in the 2000s and 2010s indicated no substantial breakthrough of the existing practice in which no strikes, go slows or collective actions for collective bargaining were officially reported.

§2. Parties to the Collective Agreement

298. For the employees' side, the trade union, represented by the trade union chairman, or representatives, elected by the employees, where there is no trade union organized, will act for the employees to conduct collective consultations and conclude the collective agreement. For the employer's side, Article 33 of the Labour Act refers only to the enterprise, whereas the Trade Union Law refers also to the institutions with enterprise-style management as a party to the collective agreement. The 2004 Regulations on Collective Agreements explicitly state that the Regulations apply to enterprises and institutions with enterprise-style management within the PRC. An enterprise will be represented or appointed by its legal person representative which is defined as the person who is in charge of and who exercises authority on behalf of a legal person according to the articles of association or according to the law.[83]

§3. Level of Bargaining and Effectiveness of the Collective Agreement

299. The practice of collective agreement was once only carried out at the enterprise level, the result being that the collective bargaining process only had effected each individual enterprise or institute which concluded such a collective agreement. Collective agreements at the mediate (professional or industrial) and national level have not been regulated explicitly in law and practice until the promulgation of the Labour Contract Law of 2007. New development has been made in the Labour Contract Law which permits the binding power of a collective agreement on the individual employment contract in industry-wide or area-wide at the county level. However, collective agreements are limited to construction, mining, catering services. Industries with significant industrial characteristics determine that they can easily enter into a feasible industry collective contract. For example, in construction and mining industries, employment of rural migrant workers is common. Personal injury or wage arrears for rural migrant workers are quite prominent problems.

82. See Fazhi Ribuo (*Legal Daily*) 20 December 1995, according to which there were 16,000 enterprises that signed collective agreements. In accordance with *Labour and Social Security in China* (White Paper), by the end of 2001 the collective agreements signed and filed with the labour authorities were 270,000.
83. See Article 38 of the General Principles of the Civil Law of the PRC.

Under the initiation of the industrial trade union, the collective contract might have played a better role in protecting the interests of migrant workers.

300. Under the 2004 Regulations on Collective Agreements, effectiveness of the collective agreement is subject to administrative review and registration. Once it is reviewed and confirmed to be satisfactory by the labour authorities, it is binding on the employer and employees together. In addition, it serves to lay down minimum norms with respect to wages, work hours, rest and leave, insurance and welfare etc. for provisions not clarified in individual labour contracts. The Labour Contract Law of 2007 appears to give more autonomy in the parties to a collective agreement which is just required to subject to filing with the labour administration. As long as no objection is received by an enterprise within 15 days upon the receipt of the agreement by the labour administration, the collective agreement submitted and filed shall become effective. In the case of the collective agreement for a specific professional or industrial sector or a region, the collective agreement shall be binding on all employers and employees in the specific professional or industrial sector or the specific region.

§4. Content of Bargaining

301. A collective agreement concerning following items or single item between parties based upon a premise of equal consultation and mutual agreement is vital for protecting collective rights.[84] The contents of the collective agreements which may be covered in the collective consultations are as follows:

(i) labour remuneration;
(ii) work hours;
(iii) rest and leave;
(iv) labour safety and health;
(v) supplementary insurance and welfare;
(vi) special protection for female workers and minors;
(vii) professional skills training;
(viii) administration of individual labour contracts;
(ix) awards and punishment;
(x) reduction of personnel;
(xi) term of collective agreements;
(xii) procedures for the modification or termination of the collective agreements;
(xiii) method for consultation to handle disputes arising through the performance of the collective agreements;
(xiv) the liability for violation of the collective agreements; and
(xv) other matters to be considered necessary by the parties to the collective agreements.

84. See Article 5 of the 2004 Regulations on Collective Agreements. In accordance with Article 52 of the Labour Contract Law, a single itemized collective agreement may cover matters such as labour safety and health; female employees' protection and adjustment mechanism for wages, etc.

302. To summarize, the content is divided into three parts. The first part concerns the norms for the minimum standards for employment and labour conditions, such as labour remuneration, working hours, rest and leave, insurance and welfare, and health and safety, etc. These are the core elements which impose the most major obligations upon the employer. The result of this part of the collective consultations would lay down the minimum standard for the provisions of individual labour contracts.

303. The second part of the consultation is about how to regulate both parties' rights and obligations with emphasis on a cooperative relationship between the trade union and the management of the enterprises. For example, in collective consultation practice, both parties may reach agreement on the production and business scale and objective of the enterprises to be achieved as a collective obligation imposed on workers. For this purpose, trade unions may undertake to make an effort with the management to fulfil agreed production targets. It is also common practice in collective consultations to determine procedures for equal consultation and discussion between two parties in dealing with disputes in the performance of the collective agreement.

304. The third part deals with general provisions in a contract regarding the duration of the contract, conditions for modifications, liabilities for breach of contract, etc. it is seen in the practice for collective agreement applicable in foreign invested companies where Chinese and certain foreign language are used at the same time as the contract languages.

305. The collective consultations in China have Chinese in characteristics. First, the agreement concluded between two parties after collective consultations only provides general terms and the written agreement often in use of standard templates. Collective consultations and agreements at the mediate (professional or industrial) and national level are still limited in legislation and practice. The Regulations on Collective Agreement and the Tentative Measures on Collective Negotiation on Salary set the norms with lower legal effect than that of the national laws and administrative regulations. Secondly, the content of the collective agreement is largely subject to state macro-planning, especially in terms of economic operation, standard of wages and employment policy. Therefore, the collective agreement is governed not only by laws and regulations but also by state plan or policy. Consequently, it leaves not too much room for negotiation between the parties to the collective agreement to detail or supplement the norms set out in labour legislation. Thirdly, the collective consultations and agreement place the emphasis on the spirit of solidarity, harmony and cooperation, to achieve the enterprise's economic objectives while the collective welfare is under the consideration.

This can be seen from the general principles or the goals of the agreement as stated in the collective agreement, as well as from provisions regarding consultation procedures for handling disputes arising through the performance of the collective agreements. Nevertheless, the recent legal provisions on collective agreements appear to encourage the collective consultation to cover more concrete issues on the collective welfare of the workers by setting up more standard norms about each items of the consultation contents as listed above.

§5. PROCEDURAL REQUIREMENTS FOR CONCLUDING A COLLECTIVE AGREEMENT

306. First, the collective agreement is to be in written form and concluded after collective consultations. No fewer than three representatives from each party with equal number of persons are to hold consultation meetings.[85] If the consultations fail, the meeting can be suspended for a duration to be agreed upon. The draft of the collective agreement is to be submitted to the workers conference or to all the staff and workers for discussion and adoption (Art. 33 of the Labour Act and Art. 51 of the Labour Contract Law).

307. Secondly, once adopted, a collective agreement is signed by the chief representative of both parties (trade union chairman or a representative appointed in writing by the trade union chairman and the legal representative of the enterprise or a manager appointed by him in writing), then it is to be submitted by the enterprise within ten days to the local labour administration for review and registration.[86] Pursuant to the 2004 Regulations on Collective Agreements, the conformity with legal requirements for the capacities of the parties to the agreement, the principle and procedures of the collective consultations and specific contents stated in the agreement will be reviewed and examined. The collective agreement will take effect if the labour administration raises no objection within 15 days after receiving the text of the collective agreement.[87] Otherwise, both parties to the collective agreement will make the necessary changes to the agreement, as suggested by the labour administration, and submit it for further review.[88]

308. Thirdly, an effective collective agreement which completed the review and registration procedure must be made public to all employees and will be binding on the enterprise and its whole staff. The term of the collective agreement shall be between one and three years, during which time both parties can examine the performance of the agreement, or revise it by means of consultation between the two parties. Any modifications or changes made must be submitted to the labour administration within 10 days for review and registration.

309. The collective agreement can be terminated due to statutory reasons (such as the dissolution and bankruptcy of an employer) or the collective agreement be terminated by agreement between both parties after consultation.

85. See Article 19 of the 2004 Regulations on Collective Agreements.
86. See Article 34 of the Labour Act, Article 42 of the 2004 Regulations on Collective Agreements.
87. See Article 34 of the Labour Act, Article 47 of the 2004 Regulations on Collective Agreements.
88. See Article 45 of the 2004 Regulations on Collective Agreements.

Chapter 4. Settlement of Disputes Arising in Collective Agreements

§1. Jurisdiction

310. Generally, the authority in charge of labour dispute settlements in labour and social security administrations at and above county level will be the regular working body for handling disputes in concluding collective agreements in the enterprises. According to Article 51 of the 2004 Regulations on Collective Agreements, territorial jurisdiction will apply to the settlement of disputes in collective consultation. The local labour authority together with the trade union organization and enterprise association at the corresponding level will carry out the conciliation for settlement of the disputes. The jurisdiction for the settlement of disputes in concluding collective agreements in enterprises that are direct subsidiaries of the central government, that are across regions, will belong to the provincial labour and social security administration designated by the Ministry of Labour and Social Security.

§2. Settlement of Disputes

311. The Labour Contract Law simply says that the trade union should apply for an arbitration and adjudication of a dispute arising from the performance of the collective agreement if negotiation fails. The 2004 Regulations on Collective Agreements were provided to apply to two kinds of dispute, namely, disputes in concluding collective agreements, i.e. disputes in collective consultations, and disputes arising in the performance of the collective agreement.

312. In handling the first kind of dispute, a written application is to be made to the labour administration for its conciliation in any dispute arising during the conclusion of the collective agreement. However, the Regulations conferred power to the labour administration, which may, according to the situation, deal with disputes without being asked to do so by the parties concerned.[89] The dispute is to be settled within 30 days of the case being received (an extra 15 days extension period can be granted), with the participation of representatives of the trade union, the enterprises association and relevant parties.[90]

313. Upon acceptance of the application for conciliation of the dispute, investigation and inquiry will be carried out. The dispute will be handled according to a plan for settlement of the dispute. An agreement on the conciliation of the dispute will be formulated and signed by the parties involved.

314. The modification and/or cancellation of the collective agreement during its term will apply procedure for collective consultation first. If there is a dispute in the collective consultation on the modification and/or termination of the collective

89. Article 49 of the 2004 Regulations on Collective Agreements.
90. Articles 50 and 51 of the 2004 Regulations on Collective Agreements.

agreement, then the conciliation procedure may be followed. This could constitute the most difficult case for conciliation in practice.

315. In settling the second kind of the dispute, i.e. disputes arising in the performance of the collective agreement, the arbitration procedures shall apply.[91] For discussion of the Regulations on the Settlement of Labour Disputes in Enterprises, see Part I Chapter 9.

§3. Strike Action

316. See the above discussion about the notion of the strikes in paragraph 259 and trade unions' role in conciliation of the work-stoppages and slow-down action above in paragraph 277.

91. Article 55 of the 2004 Regulations on Collective Agreements.

Selected Bibliography

COLLECTIONS, LAWS AND YEARBOOKS

2009 Compilation of Laws and Regulations on the Labor and Human Resources of the PRC (Law Press-China).

2017 Compilation of Laws and Regulations on the Labor and Social Security of the PRC (Law Press-China).

China Update: the PRC, Labour Law (Asia Law & Practice Ltd 1995).

The Classified Assemblage of the Law of the PRC (Law Press Beijing 1994).

Complete Book of China's Labour Law (Xinhua 1994).

Decision of the CPC Central Committee on Issues Concerning the Establishment of a Socialist Market Economic Structure in *China Daily*, 17 November 1993.

Gazette of the State Council of the PRC 1990–2017.

Labour and Social Security in China (White Paper), issued by the Information Office of the State Council of the PRC in April 2002.

The Laws of the Peoples Republic of China, Vols. 1 to 4 (for Vols. 1 to 2 Foreign Languages Press, Beijing 1987, for Vols. 3 to 4 Science Press, Beijing 1990 and 1993 respectively). (The later collection of English translation of Chinese national laws has been regularly published on an annual basis.)

Major Documents of the PRC (Foreign Languages Press, Beijing 1991).

Yearbook of Statistics of China, 1993–2017 (China Statistics Press).

Yearbook of Labour Statistics of China 1993-2016 (China Labour Publishing House).

MONOGRAPHS

Biddulph, Sarah and Cooney, Sean, 'Regulation of Trade Unions in the People's Republic of China', in *Melbourne University Law Review* Vol. 19, December 1993.

Cai and Bai (eds.) *Labor Migration in Transition China* (Social Science Academic Press 2006)

Cai, Dingjian (eds.), *The Employment Discrimination in China: Current Conditions and Anti-Discrimination Strategies* (China Social Sciences Publishing House, 2007).

Cai, Du and Wang, *How Close is China to a Labor Market* (The Commercial Press 2005).

Selected Bibliography

Chan, Antia, 'Revolution or Corporation? Workers and Trade Unions in Post-Mao China', in (1993) 19 *Australia Journal of Chinese Affairs*.

Chen, Albert H.Y., *An Introduction to the Legal System of the People's Republic of China* (Butterworths Asia 1992).

Chen, Ke, 'Role of the Trade Union in Negotiation on Collective Labour Contracts', China, in No. 48 *Bulletin of Comparative Labour Relations* (2003) Collective Bargaining, Discrimination, Social Security and European Integration, pp. 231–252.

Chen, Ke, Fixed Term Labour Contract in China, in *Fixed Term Employment Contract, A Comparative Study*, Vanden Broele 2009, pp. 161–169.

Chen, Ke, Preliminary Report on China's Rural Migrant Workers and Other Related Issues in *Diversity, Equality and Integration*, Vanden Broele 2007, pp. 91–98.

Cooney, Sean; Biddulph, Sarah and Zhu,Ying, Law and Fair Work in China: Making and Enforcing Labor Standards in the People's Republic of China (New York: Routledger, 2012).

Guan, Huai (ed.), *Labour Law Text Book* (revised version), (Mass Press 1990).

He and Zhen, 'On Chinese Characteristics of the Trade Union Law' in *Modern Law Science* No. 6 December 1992.

Jin, Qi (ed.). *Questions and Answers to the Trade Union Law-120 Issues* (Chinese People's Public Security University Press, Beijing 1992).

Josephs, Hilary K., 'Labour Reform in the Workers' State: The Chinese Experience' in *Journal of Chinese Law*, Vol. 2, Fall 1988.

Josephs, Hilary K., *Labour Law in China: Choice and Responsibility* (Butterworth legal publishers 1990).

Krieg, Renate, and Monica Schadler (eds.). *Social Security in the People's Republic of China* (Hamburg 1994).

Li, Gen, Government Regulation and Labor-capital Autonomy in Labor Relationship from the Perspective of the Court Reasonable Review of Labor Rules and Regulations, in *China Legal Science* 2016, pp.82-106.

Pan, Feng and Li, Xi-Zheng, 'Developing a System for Integrating Planned Economy with Market Regulation in China', in *Labour Markets and Human Resource Planning in Asia: Perspectives and Evidence* (ed. by M. Mugtada and A. Hildeman) ILO 1993.

Shi, Tanjin, 'On Labour Legislation and Human Rights Protection', in *Legal Studies* no. 5, 1991.

Shi, Tanjin, 'On Socialist Market Economy and Labour Legislation', in *Legal Studies* No. 1, 1994.

Wang, Bin, *A Research on the Employment Discrimination against the Citizens Who Have the Criminal Records* (China Political and Law Press, 2009).

Wang, Jianpin, 'Probe into Legal Problems of Socialist Labour Market', in *Chinese Legal Science*, No. 5, 1993 at pp. 13–18.

Yan, Tian, Revisit to the Rising of the Law against Employement Discrimination in Comtempary China, in *China Legal Science* 2016, pp. 89-121.

Ye, Jingyi (eds.) *10-year Exploration: Comparitive Study on Labor Law Reform in China and Other Countries* (Peking University Press, 2007).

Zhang, Xibo, *Labour Movement Programmes in Revolutionary Base and History of Labour Legislation* (China Labour Publishing House 1994).

Zhang, Xinguo and others, *Research on Labor Standards* (Economy & Management Publishing House 2010).

Zhu, Jia Zhen, 'On Individual Income Distribution and Social Security System', in *China Labour Newspaper* 20 January 1994 at pp. 3–4.

Selected Bibliography

Index

The numbers given refer to paragraphs.

Index

Index

Made in the USA
Monee, IL
05 November 2026

67807091R00083